T0380579

JESUS
IS THE ONLY
GOD
IN HEAVEN. . . .

THERE IS NO TRINITY GOD.

METUSELA ALBERT

To order additional copies of this book, contact:
Xlibris
844-714-8691
www.Xlibris.com
Orders@Xlibris.com

ISBN: Softcover   978-1-6641-9435-9
         EBook   978-1-6641-9435-9

Print information available on the last page

Rev. date: 09/09/2021

Contents

Introduction v

Chapter 1   The Breaking News 1

Chapter 2   Jesus Was The God (Elohim / Yahweh / Jehovah) Who Created Heaven And Earth ... 5

Chapter 3   Jesus Was The God (Elohim / Yahweh / Jehovah) Called "I Am That I Am." 9

Chapter 4   Jesus Was The God (Elohim / Yahweh / Jehovah) Who Wrote The Ten Commandments 12

Chapter 5   Jesus Was The God (Elohim / Yahweh / Jehovah) Of <u>King David</u> .... <u>14</u>

Chapter 6   Jesus Was The God (Elohim / Yahweh / Jehovah) <u>Of Prophet Isaiah</u> .... <u>17</u>

Chapter 7   Jesus Was The God (Elohim / Yahweh / Jehovah) Of <u>Prophet Daniel</u> .... <u>23</u>

Chapter 8   God (Elohim / Yahweh / Jehovah) Incarnated Into Human Flesh 27

Chapter 9   God (Elohim / Yahweh / Jehovah) Gave Birth To <u>No</u> Son In Heaven 30

Chapter 10   The Misinterpreted Text Of The Trinity Believers – Genesis 1:26 31

Chapter 11   John Advocated "<u>The Two Gods Theory</u>" Which Is Wrong – John 1:1 34

Chapter 12   John Advocated "<u>The Born Twice Theory</u>" Which Is Satanic – John 3:16 36

Chapter 13   Paul Advocated "<u>The Born Twice Theory</u>" Also Which Is Satanic 38

Chapter 14   Jesus Is The <u>Only God</u> Sitting On The Throne In Heaven – Revelation 4 42

Chapter 15   Jesus, <u>As A Human Being</u>, Was The Lamb Slain – Revelation 5 47

Chapter 16   While In Human Flesh, Jesus Had <u>Two Natures</u> (Human And Divine) 50

Chapter 17   Jesus Was The <u>Everlasting Father</u> In The Old And New Testaments 55

Chapter 18 Who Is The Holy Spirit? 60

Chapter 19 There Is Only One True God, The Father, Jesus Himself – John 17:1-5 64

Chapter 20 The Mistake Of Mrs. White And The Protestant Churches About Jesus 67

Conclusion.. 74

Introduction

I have come to realize that the vast majority who professed to believe in JESUS as the Savior and Messiah, they still do _not_ know yet that He alone was the only GOD (ELOHIM / YAHWEH / JEHOVAH) who created the heaven and the earth in six days, and rested on the seventh day – (Genesis 1:1-31; 2:1-3).

When they preached and spoke about JESUS as the Creator, they referred to Him as GOD'S begotten Son in heaven who created heaven and earth, to do the will of GOD the Father. Another expression they used for JESUS is "GOD the Son."

They spoke of GOD the Father as someone different from JESUS. And they also spoke of the Holy Spirit as a third person, different from the Father and JESUS.

They also believed that JESUS existed in heaven as GOD'S Son before the angels' existed. In other words, they believed that GOD the Father _gave birth_ to a begotten Son in heaven and called his name JESUS before the angels existed. That is what they expressed in their beliefs about JESUS.

1. They did not know that JESUS was the Almighty, self-existent GOD (Elohim / Yahweh / Jehovah) who created heaven and earth who became the Almighty God of Abraham, Isaac, and Jacob, who later became incarnated into human flesh at Bethlehem through Mary, to die at Calvary as our Sin Bearer.

2. They did not know that JESUS was _not_ the Son of GOD in heaven prior to the incarnation at Bethlehem.

3. They did not know that GOD the Father had no begotten Son in heaven called JESUS before the angels existed.

4. Of course, most Protestant Churches of today still don't know yet that JESUS was the Almighty GOD of Abraham, Isaac, and Jacob, who later became incarnated into human flesh at Bethlehem through Mary, and is called – JESUS, the Son of GOD.

5. JESUS was not called "GOD the Son." There is no such thing as "GOD the Son" existed in heaven before the angels existed.

6. The phrase – JESUS as "the Son of GOD" only existed when He was born by Mary at Bethlehem.

7. Without the incarnation of YAHWEH (JEHOVAH) into human flesh, there would have been <u>no</u> Son of God. . . . JESUS is <u>not</u> "GOD the Son."

8. And there is <u>no</u> such thing as a Trinity GOD <u>nor</u> a Triune GOD.

HERE IS THE REAL TRUTH ABOUT JESUS:

JESUS was only being called "<u>the Son of GOD</u>" when YAHWEH (JEHOVAH) was incarnated into human flesh through Mary at Bethlehem around 04 B.C. - (Luke 1:35). That is the only time that JESUS was literally born because of the incarnation process He took to become human flesh, <u>to enable Him to die</u> at Calvary as our Sin Bearer. The immortal Creator (YAHWEH / JEHOVAH) voluntarily became our mortal Sin Bearer.

In fact, JESUS was <u>never</u> born in heaven. <u>No GOD in heaven literally gave birth to a literal Son before the angels existed</u>.

JESUS was ELOHIM, YAHWEH, JEHOVAH, the <u>only everlasting self-existent GOD</u>, the Alpha and Omega, who had <u>no</u> beginning and <u>no</u> ending.

....

PLEASE TAKE NOTE OF THESE IMPORTANT TRUTHS BELOW ABOUT JESUS:

1. It was GOD / ELOHIM / YAHWEH / JEHOVAH who humbly became human flesh at Bethlehem through Mary and is called – JESUS, the Son of GOD.

2. It was <u>NOT</u> the Son of GOD who became human flesh at Bethlehem.

3. There was <u>NO</u> Son of GOD in heaven before the angels existed.

4. There was <u>NO</u> Trinity God in heaven.

5. There was <u>NO</u> three persons that existed in heaven before the angels existed

Dear reader, how would a person know the error if he or she did <u>not</u> know who JESUS was in the Old Testament? Of course, that person cannot know the error written by John and Paul in the New Testament.

First, we need to know the real truth about who JESUS was in the Old Testament, then we can detect the errors made by the disciples and Paul, in their writings in the New Testament.

The *TRINITY GOD theory* which is the *TRIUNE GOD theory* is the error that is attacking the self-existence of JESUS who was GOD / ELOHIM / YAHWEH / JEHOVAH before the angels were created by Him.

NOTE: If you believed in the TRINITY doctrine, then you would have to believe also that JESUS was <u>not</u> the self-existent GOD that created heaven and earth. And you would have to believe that the Father literally gave birth to a Son in heaven before the angels existed. And you would have to also believe that the two of them existed in heaven before the angels were created, but the Father existed *first* before the Son was begotten by Him (the Father).

Therefore, if you believed that JESUS was the begotten Son of GOD the Father in heaven called "<u>GOD the Son</u>," then you are advocating a theology of <u>TWO DISTINCT GODS</u> without you realizing it.

Furthermore, if you are advocating a third person in heaven called – "GOD the Holy Spirit," then you are promoting the "<u>THREE GODS</u>" theory which is Satanic.

THIS BOOK HAD TO BE WRITTEN

Since the lie is so subtle and is creating so much confusion, I decided to write this book as <u>THE BREAKING NEWS</u> for Christianity, in order to counteract the false teaching that is permeating and corrupting the Protestant Churches.

I urge you to continue reading this book, and after this, you need to share it with your friends to stop the lies of Satan. The truth must be promoted to exalt JESUS, who is our only God in heaven.

. . . .

CHAPTER 1

THE BREAKING NEWS

JESUS IS THE ONLY GOD IN HEAVEN. . . . THERE IS NO TRINITY GOD.

1. There is **no** other GOD besides JESUS in heaven. JESUS alone is sitting on the throne - (Isaiah 43:10, 44:6, 24; 49:16; Revelation 4:1-11).

2. Worship is due to JESUS alone because He was the Creator who became our Savior in human flesh like us - (Exodus 20:1-3; Revelation 14:6-7; Hebrews 2:14-17; 4:15).

3. JESUS was the "ELOHIM / YAHWEH / JEHOVAH" who created heaven and earth - (Genesis 1:1-31; 2:1-3; Isaiah 44:6, 24; 49:16).

4. JESUS was the ELOHIM / YAHWEH / JEHOVAH called - "I AM THAT I AM" who spoke to Moses at the burning bush - (Exodus 3:13-14; 6:1-3; John 8:58).

5. JESUS was the "ELOHIM / YAHWEH / JEHOVAH" who delivered the children of Israel from slavery in Egypt - (Exodus 6:1-3; 20:1-3).

6. JESUS was the ELOHIM / YAHWEH / JEHOVAH who wrote the Ten Commandments and gave them through Moses - (Exodus 6:1-3; 20:1-3; John 14:15).

7. JESUS was the ELOHIM / YAHWEH / JEHOVAH who became incarnated into human flesh and is called JESUS, the Son of GOD - (Isaiah 7:14; 9:6; Matthew 1:21-23; Luke 1:35).

8. JESUS was called – The Son of God at Bethlehem; **not** God the Son.

9. JESUS was the everlasting Father in the Old and New Testaments - (Isaiah 9:6; Psalm 90:1-2).

10. JESUS was the Father that spoke from heaven at the baptism - (Matthew 3:17; Luke 3:22).

11. JESUS was the GOD of Prophet Isaiah called "the First and the Last" who spoke to John on the Island of Patmos - (Isaiah 44:6, 24; Revelation 1:9-11; 17:18; 21:6-7).

12. JESUS was the Father while in human flesh. He spoke to Phillip and declared him as the Father – (John 14:6-9).

13. In His conversation with Satan, JESUS told him that He is the LORD GOD and worship is due to Him – (Matthew 4:7-10).

14. JESUS is the only GOD sitting on the Throne in heaven - (Revelation 4:1-11).

15. JESUS is coming back as KING of kings and LORD of lords - (Revelation 19:1-10).

NOTE: When YAHWEH took human flesh by the incarnation process and was born of Mary at Bethlehem as the holy one called JESUS, the Jews failed to understand his prophecy about Himself in the Book of Isaiah. (Isaiah 43:10; 44:6, 24; 49:16; 9:6; 7:14).

The Jews were correct in believing that God alone can forgive sins – (Mark 2:1-10). But they *failed* to realize that JESUS who is in human flesh, born of Mary, can forgive sins because He is God. They could not accept Jesus as God because to them, that would make Two Gods since they knew there is only one God in the Torah which is the Almighty God of Abraham.

However, they did not realize that JESUS was the "Elohim" mentioned in the Torah. They did not know that JESUS was the Almighty God of Abraham in the Torah.

TAKE NOTE OF THIS CRUCIAL POINT:

We who professed to be Christians must not get confused like the Jews did 2,000 years ago and killed JESUS at Calvary - 31 A.D. When they killed JESUS, they did not kill GOD because GOD cannot die. GOD is immortal.

They only killed His incarnated body in human flesh which is a *mortal* body like ours.

Therefore, understanding the *two natures* of JESUS while he was in human flesh, is vital. You need to read Chapter 16 of this Book and share it with your friends.

. . . .

THE BREAKING NEWS

1. It was GOD / ELOHIM / YAHWEH / JEHOVAH who humbly became human flesh at Bethlehem through Mary and is called – JESUS, the Son of GOD - (Isaiah 9:6; 7:14; Luke 1:35; Matthew 1:21-23).

2. It was <u>NOT</u> the Son of GOD who became human flesh at Bethlehem.

3. There was <u>NO</u> Son of GOD in heaven before the angels existed.

JESUS ALONE IS GOD. HE IS TO BE WORSHIPPED.

Therefore, there is <u>no</u> such thing called - a Trinity God or a Triune God. There is <u>no</u> such thing as - three in one (1 + 1 + 1 = 1).

The Trinity doctrine is a HOAX. . . . Of course, the Trinity doctrine is Anti-Christ.

Yea, the Trinity doctrine degrades JESUS who is an eternal God to become a creature, a Son of God in heaven, born of God the Father in heaven before the angels existed. . . . The Trinity doctrine is Satanic.

The Trinity doctrine promotes the notion that JESUS was born twice; born of God the Father in heaven, and born of Mary on earth. That doctrine is truly Satanic.

. . . .

WHAT ABOUT THE HOLY SPIRIT?

The Holy Spirit is the Spirit of GOD which is the Spirit of JESUS. Since JESUS is the only GOD in heaven, therefore, when you sin against the Holy Spirit which is the Spirit of JESUS, thus, you are sinning against JESUS who is our only GOD. Please Read Chapter 17 of this Book.

. . . .

THE HOLY SPIRIT IS <u>NOT</u> A THIRD PERSON IN HEAVEN.

There is only one God in heaven; <u>not</u> two <u>nor</u> three.

JESUS is the only God in heaven. He became human flesh to enable him to die at Calvary as our Sin Bearer / Savior.

If God (Elohim / Yahweh / Jehovah) did not incarnate into human flesh, then we would have no one to pay for our penalty of sin. The angels cannot. It had to be Elohim / Yahweh / Jehovah himself to atone for our sins.

God / Elohim / Yahweh / Jehovah taking upon himself human flesh to die at Calvary to atone for our sins, reveals the greatness of His love toward us so that none should be lost eternally, but all should come in repentance and be saved from sin and eternal destruction - (2 Peter 3:9-10). This is the amazing love of JESUS who is our God.

//

There is <u>no</u> second person <u>nor</u> a third person of the Godhead in heaven.

In heaven, JESUS alone is God. His Spirit is called the Holy Spirit.

. . . .

THE GODHEAD IS MADE UP OF <u>ONE</u> GOD, AND HE IS JESUS.

The Godhead is <u>not</u> made up of three distinct gods.

There is <u>NO</u> such thing as: God the Father + God the Son + God the Holy Spirit = 1 GOD.

Read <u>CHAPTER 18</u> of this book about the Holy Spirit. Thank you.

. . . .

CHAPTER 2

JESUS WAS THE GOD (ELOHIM / YAHWEH / JEHOVAH) WHO CREATED HEAVEN AND EARTH

SCRIPTURE:

Genesis 1:1 - In the beginning <u>God</u> created the heaven and the earth. (KJV).

. . . .

The Bible begins by introducing <u>God</u> as the Creator of heaven and earth - (Genesis 1:1). The word "God" in English refers to a divine being which is Omnipotent (all powerful), Omnipresent (can be present anywhere), and Omniscient (all knowing).

NOTE: The Creator was <u>not</u> the Son of God <u>nor</u> God the Son. This point must be understood from the very beginning to avoid misinterpretation of Scripture; for there is <u>no such thing</u> as a Trinity God created heaven and earth.

The God (Elohim) who created heaven and earth that you read in Genesis 1:1 was the same one who created the light in Genesis 1:3.

WHO WAS THIS "<u>GOD</u>" WHO CREATED THE LIGHT IN GENESIS 1:3?

And <u>GOD said</u>, "Let there be light"; and there was light.

In the New Testament, <u>JESUS said</u>, "<u>I am</u> the light of the world" (John 8:12).

Of course, JESUS was the ELOHIM / YAHWEH (JEHOVAH) who created the light in Genesis 1:3. He was the Creator introduced in Genesis 1:1.

JESUS WAS THE GOD (ELOHIM / YAHWEH / ALLAH / JEHOVAH) WHO CREATED THE LIGHT IN GENESIS 1:3.

Genesis 1:1 – "In the beginning <u>God</u> created the heaven and the earth."

Genesis 1:3 – <u>God said</u>, "Let there be light; ."

John 8:12 - - <u>Jesus said</u>, "<u>I am the light of the world</u>: he that followeth me shall not walk in darkness, but shall have the light of life.

John 8:58 – Jesus said, ". . . Before Abraham was, I am."

JESUS was the ELOHIM / YAHWEH / JEHOVAH that spoke to the Prophets in the Old Testament era – (Exodus 3:13-14; 6:1-3; Isaiah 26:4; Psalms 88:13). ELOHIM <u>did not</u> have a Son called JESUS in the Old Testament time.

THERE IS NO SUCH THING AS A TRINITY GOD CREATED HEAVEN AND EARTH.

Look at the pronoun "he" in Genesis 1:5.

Genesis 1:1   -5 - KJV

- 1 - In the beginning   <u>God</u> created the heaven and the earth.
- 2 And the earth was without form, and void; and darkness was upon the face of the deep. And   <u>the Spirit of God</u>   moved upon the face of the waters.

- 3 And <u>God said, Let there be light</u>   : and there was light.
- 4 And <u>God saw</u> the light, that it was good: and   <u>God</u> divided the light from the darkness.

- 5 And <u>God called</u>   the light Day, and the darkness   <u>he</u> called Night. And   <u>the evening and the morning were the first day</u> .

IF you need further information about the Almighty God of Abraham, I recommend that you try and acquire the Book below called – "JESUS was the Almighty God of Abraham."

www.metuselaalbert.com

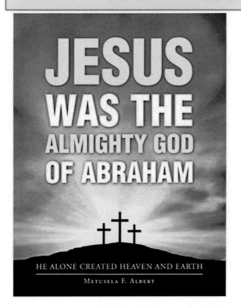

WHAT IS THE TRUTH?

• Most Professed Christians and Protestant Churches have not understood yet that JESUS who became our Sin Bearer at Calvary (31 A.D.) was the Almighty God of Abraham who created heaven and earth.

1 THE CREATOR – YAHWEH / JEHOVAH / ELOHIM

2 BECAME THE ALMIGHTY GOD OF ABRAHAM AND THE CHILDREN OF ISRAEL

3 HE HUMBLY INCARNATED INTO HUMAN FLESH AND IS CALLED "JESUS OF NAZARETH," THE FIRST AND THE LAST, THE KING OF THE JEWS, ALPHA AND OMEGA, THE SON OF GOD AND YET HE WAS THE ONLY EVERLASTING GOD WHO MADE HEAVEN AND EARTH.

Read: Genesis 1:1, 3-5, 31; 2:1-3; Exodus 3:13-14; 6:1-3; Isaiah 26:4; 44:6, 24; 49:16; 9:6; 7:14; John 5:39, 46; 8:12, 56-58; Matthew 1:21-23; Luke 1:35; Revelation 1:17-18; 21:6-7.

POWERPOINT SLIDE PREPARED BY: METUSELA F. ALBERT

THINK SERIOUSLY ABOUT THIS.

When we come to a full understanding that <u>the God of prophet Isaiah</u> who <u>created heaven and earth was Jesus,</u> we then become convinced that <u>there is only one God in heaven.</u>

THE GOD WHO SPOKE TO PROPHET ISAIAH IS THE ONLY ONE GOD IN HEAVEN. HE IS JESUS!

- Isaiah 43:10
- [10] Ye are my witnesses, <u>saith the Lord</u>, and my servant whom I have chosen: that ye may know and believe me, and understand that **I am he:** before me there was no God formed, neither shall there be after me.

ONLY ONE GOD

- Isaiah 44:6
- [6] Thus saith the Lord the King of Israel, and his redeemer the Lord of hosts; <u>I am the first, and I am the last; and</u> **beside me there is no God**.
- Isaiah 44:24

THE REDEEMER IS THE CREATOR, THE FIRST AND THE LAST.

- [24] Thus saith the Lord, thy redeemer, and he that formed thee from the womb, <u>I am the Lord that maketh all things</u>; that stretcheth forth the heavens **alone**; that spreadeth abroad the earth by **myself**;

- Isaiah 49:16

THE PROPHECY OF HIS DEATH AT CALVARY

- [16] Behold, **I have graven thee upon the palms of my hands** ; thy walls are continually before me.

THIS IS NOT A TRINITY GOD NOR A TRIUNE GOD

The conversation between God and prophet Isaiah in the Scriptures shown above should help us understand what Jesus said of Himself in His conversation with others in the New Testament.

For example, JESUS said – "Before Abraham was, I am." (John 8:58).

Another example, JESUS said – "Had you believed Moses, you would have believed me; <u>for Moses wrote about me</u>." (John 5:46).

Understanding who JESUS was in the Old Testament, that should help us easily recognize <u>the errors of the disciples in their beliefs about who Jesus was in the Old Testament.</u>

Therefore, the only <u>logical conclusion</u> is – THERE IS <u>NO</u> TRINITY GOD IN HEAVEN.

. . . .

CHAPTER 3

JESUS WAS THE GOD (ELOHIM / YAHWEH / JEHOVAH) CALLED "I AM THAT I AM."

Exodus 3:13-14

[13] And <u>Moses said unto God</u>, "Behold, when I come unto the children of Israel and shall say unto them, 'The God of your fathers hath sent me unto you,' and they shall say to me, '<u>What is His name?'</u> <u>what shall I say unto them</u>?"

[14] And <u>God said unto Moses</u>, "<u>I Am That I Am</u>." And He said, "Thus shalt thou say unto the children of Israel, 'I Am hath sent me unto you.'"

. . . .

John 8:58

[58] <u>Jesus said unto them</u>, "Verily, verily I say unto you, <u>before Abraham was, I am</u>!"

///

JESUS WAS "THE I AM THAT I AM" WHO SPOKE TO MOSES AT THE BURNING BUSH.

- Scripture:
-
- Exodus 3:13-14

- [13] And <u>Moses said unto God</u>, "Behold, when I come unto the children of Israel and shall say unto them, 'The God of your fathers hath sent me unto you,' and they shall say to me, '<u>What is His name?' what shall I say unto them?</u>"

-
- [14] And <u>God said unto Moses, "I AM THAT I AM." And He said, "Thus shalt thou say unto the children of Israel, I AM hath sent me unto you.</u>'"

-
- John 8:58

- [58] <u>Jesus said unto them,</u> "Verily, verily I say unto you, <u>before Abraham was, I am!</u>"

-

•THE GOD OF ABRAHAM, ISAAC, AND JACOB CALLED – "I AM THAT I AM," HE IS JESUS.

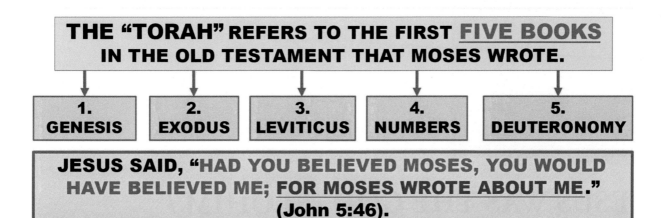

THE "TORAH" REFERS TO THE FIRST FIVE BOOKS IN THE OLD TESTAMENT THAT MOSES WROTE.

| 1. GENESIS | 2. EXODUS | 3. LEVITICUS | 4. NUMBERS | 5. DEUTERONOMY |

JESUS SAID, "HAD YOU BELIEVED MOSES, YOU WOULD HAVE BELIEVED ME; FOR MOSES WROTE ABOUT ME."
(John 5:46).

JESUS WAS THE ELOHIM / YAHWEH / JEHOVAH / GOD OF ABRAHAM WHO CREATED HEAVEN AND EARTH IN SIX DAYS AND RESTED ON THE SEVENTH DAY, THAT YOU READ IN THE TORAH. JESUS IS NOT A TRINITY GOD.

///

CHAPTER 4

JESUS WAS THE GOD (ELOHIM / YAHWEH / JEHOVAH) WHO WROTE THE TEN COMMANDMENTS

Exodus 20:1-3

> • **JESUS WAS THE GOD (ELOHIM / YAHWEH / JEHOVAH) WHO WROTE THE TEN COMMANDMENTS.**
> •
> • **Scripture:**
> •
> • **Exodus 20:1-3**
> • **1. And God spake all these words, saying,**
>
> • **² I am the LORD thy God, which have brought thee out of the land of Egypt, out of the house of bondage.**
>
> • **³ Thou shalt have no other gods before me.**
>
> **THIS WAS NOT A TRINITY GOD. . .Look at the Singular PRONOUN.**

John 14:15 – In the New Testament, JESUS said, "If you love me, keep my commandments."

JESUS was the Elohim / Yahweh / Jehovah who wrote the Ten Commandments and gave through Moses at Mount Sinai for all mankind.

•THE GOD OF ABRAHAM, ISAAC, AND JACOB CALLED – "I AM THAT I AM," HE IS JESUS.

//

- JESUS IS <u>NOT</u> A TRINITY GOD.

- JESUS IS <u>NOT</u> A TRIUNE GOD.

- JESUS IS <u>NOT</u> A SECOND PERSON OF THE GODHEAD.

- JESUS IS <u>NOT</u> GOD THE SON.

CHAPTER 5

JESUS WAS THE GOD (ELOHIM / YAHWEH / JEHOVAH) OF <u>KING DAVID</u>

SCRIPTURE:

Psalm 23:1-6

1. <u>The LORD is my shepherd</u>; I shall not want.

² He maketh me to lie down in green pastures; He leadeth me beside the still waters.

³ He restoreth my soul; He leadeth me in the paths of righteousness for His name's sake.

⁴ Yea, though I walk through the valley of the shadow of death, I will fear no evil; for Thou art with me; Thy rod and Thy staff, they comfort me.

⁵ Thou preparest a table before me in the presence of mine enemies; Thou anointest my head with oil; my cup runneth over.

⁶ Surely goodness and mercy shall follow me all the days of my life; and I will dwell in the house of <u>the LORD</u> for ever.

. . . .

Psalm 90:1-2

1. <u>LORD,</u> Thou hast been our dwelling place in all generations.

² Before the mountains were brought forth, or ever <u>Thou hadst formed the earth and the world, even from everlasting to everlasting, Thou art God</u>.

. . . .

Psalm 95:3-6

³ For <u>the Lord is a great God</u>, and <u>a great King</u> above all gods.

⁴ In His hand are the deep places of the earth; the strength of the hills is His also.

⁵ The sea is His, and <u>He made it; and His hands formed the dry land.</u>

⁶ <u>O come, let us worship and bow down; let us kneel before the Lord our Maker</u>.

. . . .

PSALM 100:3

³ Know ye that <u>the Lord, He is God; it is He that hath made us</u>, and not we ourselves. We are His people, and <u>the sheep of His pasture</u>.

. . . .

Psalm 18:1-2

1. I will love Thee, <u>O Lord</u>, my strength.

² <u>The Lord is my rock and my fortress and my deliverer; my God, my strength</u>, <u>in whom I will trust</u>; my buckler, and the horn of <u>my salvation, and my high tower.</u>

. . . .

NEW TESTAMENT

John 10:10-14 - King James Version

¹⁰ The thief cometh not but to steal and to kill and to destroy. I am come that they might have life, and that they might have it more abundantly.

¹¹ <u>I am the Good Shepherd</u>; the Good Shepherd giveth His life for the sheep.

¹² But he that is a hireling and not the shepherd, whose own the sheep are not, seeth the wolf coming and leaveth the sheep and fleeth; and the wolf catcheth them and scattereth the sheep.

¹³ The hireling fleeth because he is a hireling, and careth not for the sheep.

¹⁴ <u>I am the Good Shepherd</u>, and know My sheep and am known by Mine.

. . . .

1 Corinthians 10:1-4

10 Moreover, brethren, I would not have ye ignorant of how all of our fathers were under the cloud, and all passed through the sea,

² and all were baptized unto Moses in the cloud and in the sea.

³ And all ate the same spiritual meat,

⁴ and all drank the same spiritual drink; for they drank of that spiritual Rock that followed them, and that Rock was Christ.

. . . .

EXPLANATION

King David calls the LORD his Shepherd.

In the New Testament, JESUS says that He is the good Shepherd.

JESUS was the Rock of David. HE was the shield for David while King Saul seeks to kill him.

Of course, YAHWEH (JEHOVAH) was the everlasting God of King David and the children of Israel in the Old Testament. They knew only one God.

They did not know that the one God they professed to serve is JESUS. The name JESUS only came about in the New Testament which refers to the God of the prophets in the Old Testament and the children of Israel.

. . . .

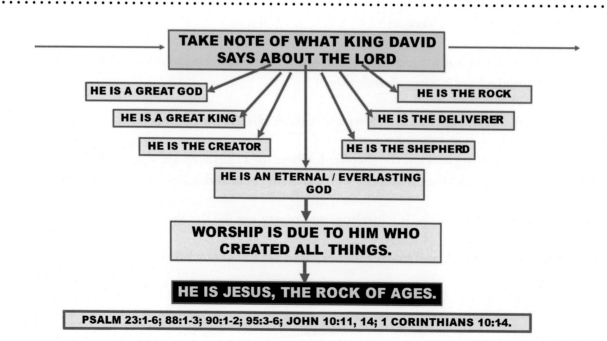

CHAPTER 6

JESUS WAS THE GOD (ELOHIM / YAHWEH / JEHOVAH) <u>OF PROPHET ISAIAH</u>

When we come to a better understanding that <u>the God of Prophet Isaiah who created heaven and earth was JESUS</u>, we then become fully convinced that there is <u>only one God</u> in heaven.

Therefore, the only logical conclusion is – THERE IS <u>NO</u> TRINITY GOD IN HEAVEN.

THIS IS NOT A TRINITY GOD. READ THE SINGULAR PRONOUN.

- Isaiah 41:10 – (King James Version)

- "Fear thou not; for I am with thee: be not dismayed; for I am thy God: I will strengthen thee; yea, I will help thee; yea, I will uphold thee with the right hand of my righteousness."

There is <u>only one God</u> in heaven. He tells prophet Isaiah that he alone is God. Read the <u>pronouns</u> that are in <u>singular</u> form; <u>not</u> in <u>plural</u> form.

Well, let's read the Scriptures. Isaiah 43:10; 44:6, 24; 49:16.

THE GOD WHO SPOKE TO PROPHET ISAIAH IS THE ONLY ONE GOD IN HEAVEN. NONE BEFORE HIM AND NONE AFTER HIM.   HE IS JESUS!

- Isaiah 43:10
- [10] Ye are my witnesses, saith the LORD, and my servant whom I have chosen: that ye may know and believe me, and understand that I am he: before me there was no God formed, neither shall there be after me.

ONLY ONE GOD

- Isaiah 44:6
- [6] Thus saith the LORD the King of Israel, and his redeemer the LORD of hosts; I am the first, and I am the last; and beside me there is no God.

ONLY ONE GOD

- Isaiah 44:24

THE REDEEMER IS THE CREATOR, THE FIRST AND THE LAST.

- [24] Thus saith the LORD, thy redeemer, and he that formed thee from the womb, I am the LORD that maketh all things; that stretcheth forth the heavens alone; that spreadeth abroad the earth by myself;

- Isaiah 49:16

THE PROPHECY OF HIS DEATH AT CALVARY

- [16] Behold, I have graven thee upon the palms of my hands thy walls are continually before me.

THIS WAS NOT A TRINITY GOD NOR A TRIUNE GOD

The same God who spoke to Prophet Isaiah spoke to all the Prophets in the Old Testament. He wrote the Ten Commandments and gave to Moses for all mankind. In fact, the Ten Commandments were written before the time of Prophet Isaiah.

SCRIPTURE:

Exodus 20:1-3 - King James Version

1. And God spake all these words, saying,

2. I am the LORD thy God, which have brought thee out of the land of Egypt, out of the house of bondage.

3. Thou shalt have no other gods before me.

. . . .

EXPLANATION

The God who spoke and wrote the Ten Commandments was <u>not</u> a Trinity God.

Did you notice the <u>pronouns</u> used in the above Scripture? . . . A <u>singular</u> pronoun. Read the Scripture, and see it for yourself.

> • **JESUS WAS THE GOD (ELOHIM / YAHWEH / JEHOVAH) WHO WROTE THE TEN COMMANDMENTS.**
> •
> • **Scripture:**
> •
> • **Exodus 20:1-3**
> • **1. And <u>God</u> spake all these words, saying,**
>
> • **² I am the LORD thy God, which have brought thee out of the land of Egypt, out of the house of bondage.**
>
> • **³ Thou shalt have no other gods before <u>me</u>.**
>
> **THIS WAS NOT A TRINITY GOD. . .Look at the Singular PRONOUN.**

If the <u>first commandment</u> shown above did not convince you, then let us read the <u>fourth</u> commandment, and prove it further that there was <u>no</u> Trinity God. The <u>fourth</u> commandment is about the Sabbath day.

Exodus 20:8-11 - King James Version

⁸ Remember <u>the sabbath day</u>, to keep it holy.

⁹ Six days shalt thou labour, and do all thy work:

¹⁰ But <u>the seventh day is the sabbath</u> of <u>the LORD thy God</u>: in it thou shalt not do any work, thou, nor thy son, nor thy daughter, thy manservant, nor thy maidservant, nor thy cattle, nor thy stranger that is within thy gates:

¹¹ For in six days <u>the LORD</u> made heaven and earth, the sea, and all that in them is, and rested the seventh day: wherefore <u>the LORD</u> blessed the sabbath day, and hallowed it.

. . . .

Genesis 2:1-3 (King James Version).

1. Thus the heavens and the earth were finished, and all the host of them.

² And on the seventh day God ended his work which he had made; and he rested on the seventh day from all his work which he had made.

³ And God blessed the seventh day, and sanctified it: because that in it he had rested from all his work which God created and made.

. . . .

PLEASE TAKE NOTE OF THE SINGULAR PRONOUN OF THE MALE GENDER GOD IN THE SCRIPTURE – GENESIS 2:1-3.

The God who created heaven and earth in six days rested on the seventh day from all his work which he had made.

It is very clear - That God mentioned in Genesis 2:1-3 who gave the Sabbath day to Adam and Eve was not a Trinity God. HE was the same God who wrote the Ten Commandments at Mount Sinai.

THE SEVENTH DAY OF THE WEEK IS THE SABBATH DAY. . . .
(Genesis 2:1-3; Exodus 20:8-11).
JESUS IS THE LORD OF THE SABBATH DAY.

NO TRINITY GOD CREATED THE SABBATH DAY.

- Genesis 2:1-3 King James Version
- 1. Thus the heavens and the earth were finished, and all the host of them.
- ² And on the seventh day God ended his work which he had made; and he rested on the seventh day from all his work which he had made.
- ³ And God blessed the seventh day, and sanctified it: because that in it he had rested from all his work which God created and made.

Further Reading: Mark 2:27-28; Luke 4:16; 23:54-56; 24:1-5; Revelation 14:6-7; 22:14; Ecclesiastes 12:13-14.

Of course, Saturday is the Sabbath day. It is the day *after* Friday; and it is the day *before* Sunday.

Sunday is the *first day* of the week. Sunday is <u>not</u> the Sabbath day. Sunday is the day after the Sabbath day.

In the year 31 A.D., JESUS died <u>on a Friday</u>, rested in the grave on the Sabbath day, and rose from the grave on a Sunday. JESUS destroyed the enemy called – "Death," so that none should die <u>the eternal death</u> which is <u>the second death</u>.

Remember, <u>nobody inherited</u> eternal death from Adam. And nobody was born with Adam's sin. Of course, <u>nobody inherited</u> Adam's sin.

No baby inherited Adam's sin. We only inherited a fallen sinful nature which is <u>not</u> sin in itself. The fallen sinful nature does <u>not</u> make a baby a sinner in the mother's womb. For "sin is the transgression of God's law" – 1 John 3:4. (Read Romans 3:20 and 4:15).

JESUS did <u>not</u> inherit Adam's sin. HE died the eternal death as if he was the guilty sinner, to atone for our sins. This is the amazing love of JESUS, our only GOD in heaven. JESUS voluntarily became sin for us, yet not a sinner. He was tempted in all points like as we are, yet sinned not – (Hebrews 4:15). Thank you, JESUS.

JESUS IS ALIVE FOREVER MOR E.

THE SAME GOD WHO SPOKE TO PROPHET ISAIAH REVEALED HIMSELF TO JOHN ON THE ISLAND OF PATMOS. HE IS THE FIRST AND THE LAST. HE IS JESUS.

JESUS WAS THE GOD OF PROPHET ISAIAH, CALLED – THE FIRST AND THE LAST, THE ALPHA AND OMEGA.
HE SPOKE TO JOHN ON THE ISLAND OF PATMOS.

Scripture:

Isaiah 44:6 – Thus saith the Lord the King of Israel, and his redeemer the Lord of hosts; I am the first, and I am the last; and beside me there is no God.

Revelation 21:6-7

⁶ And he (JESUS) said unto me (John), It is done. I am Alpha and Omega, the beginning and the end . I will give unto him that is athirst of the fountain of the water of life freely.
⁷ He that overcometh shall inherit all things; and I will be his God , and he shall be my son.

Further Reading - Revelation 1:9-11, 17-18.

JESUS IS THE ONLY GOD IN HEAVEN.

THE GOD WHO SPOKE TO PROPHET ISAIAH IS THE ONLY ONE GOD IN HEAVEN.   HE IS JESUS!

- Isaiah 43:10
- ¹⁰ Ye are my witnesses, saith the LORD, and my servant whom I have chosen: that ye may know and believe me, and understand that I am he: before me there was no God formed, neither shall there be after me.
- Isaiah 44:6   **ONLY ONE GOD**
- ⁶ Thus saith the LORD the King of Israel, and his redeemer the LORD of hosts; I am the first, and I am the last; and beside me there is no God.
- Isaiah 44:24   **THE REDEEMER IS THE CREATOR, THE FIRST AND THE LAST.**
- ²⁴ Thus saith the LORD, thy redeemer, and he that formed thee from the womb, I am the LORD that maketh all things; that stretcheth forth the heavens alone; that spreadeth abroad the earth by myself;
- Isaiah 49:16   **THE PROPHECY OF JESUS' DEATH AT CALVARY**
- ¹⁶ Behold, I have graven thee upon the palms of my hands; thy walls are continually before me.

THIS IS NOT A TRINITY GOD NOR A TRIUNE GOD

THE PROPHETS AND THE CHILDREN OF ISRAEL KNEW ONLY ONE GOD; NOT A TRINITY GOD.

DURING THE TIME OF JESUS ON EARTH, THE JEWS DID NOT KNOW THAT JESUS WHO WAS BORN OF MARY AT BETHLEHEM WAS THE GOD OF ABRAHAM, ISAAC, AND JACOB THE GOD OF ABRAHAM, ISAAC, AND JACOB IN THE OLD TESTAMENT.

THEY FAILED TO UNDERSTAND THE BOOK OF ISAIAH.

WHEN THE JEWS KILLED JESUS AT CALVARY THROUGH THE ROMAN SOLDIERS, THEY FULFILLED THE PROPHECY IN ISAIAH 53:10.

TODAY, PROTESTANT CHURCHES OF THE 21 ST CENTURY (A.D.) INCLUDING THE SDA CHURCH FAILED TO UNDERSTAND WHO JESUS WAS AND IS.

JESUS WAS THE YAHWEH (JEHOVAH) WHO WROTE THE TEN COMMANDMENTS.

JESUS IS THE ONLY GOD IN HEAVEN. HE IS NOT A TRINITY GOD.

CHAPTER 7

JESUS WAS THE GOD (ELOHIM / YAHWEH / JEHOVAH) OF <u>PROPHET DANIEL</u>

Daniel lived around the time of King Nebuchadnezzar of Babylon. He was the author of the Book of Daniel in the Bible. In Daniel <u>Chapter 2</u>, we read the story of Nebuchadnezzar's forgotten dream.

One day the King had a dream that troubled him. In the morning, he forgot the dream. Well, he called all the wise men of his country to tell him of his dream. Because none could tell what king dreamt, he ordered that all his Counsellors / Advisers should be killed.

At this time, Daniel was in Babylon as one of the Jewish prisoners. The death decree affected Daniel. So, Daniel asked if time could be extended since he and his three friends would fast and pray to their God to reveal this secret thing. And the God of the children of Israel answered their prayers.

Then Daniel was taken to the King to tell the dream and the interpretation. God not only revealed the dream <u>but also gave the meaning of the dream</u>.

THIS WAS THE DREAM.

1. An <u>image</u> like a person that is made up of different medals.

2. The head of the image is made of <u>gold</u>.

3. The arms and breast are made of <u>silver</u>.

4. The thighs are made of <u>bronze</u>.

5. The legs are made of <u>iron</u>.

6. The feet and ten toes are made of <u>iron and clay</u>.

7. Then <u>a stone</u> was cast and it came and hit the image <u>at the feet of iron and clay</u>.

8. The stone became a nation that cannot be destroyed.

9. The dream is about the future and is certain.

THE MEANING OF THE DREAM.

1. The head of gold refers to king Nebuchadnezzar of Babylon.

2. After Babylon, another nation symbolized by the silver would arise.

3. And another third (bronze) nation and fourth nation (iron) to follow.

4. Then during the time of the iron and clay (the feet and toes), the Stone which represents <u>the second coming of JESUS</u> would take place.

. . . .

- 38 And wheresoever the children of men dwell, the beasts of the field and the fowls of the heaven hath he given into thine hand, and hath made thee ruler over them all. <u>Thou art this head of gold.</u>

- 39 And <u>after thee shall arise another kingdom inferior to thee, and another third kingdom of brass,</u> which shall bear rule over all the earth.

The key point for interpreting the Dream is in Daniel 2:38-39.

THE FULFILLMENT OF THE DREAM FROM THE TIME OF BABYLON.

1. HEAD OF <u>GOLD</u> – BABYLON – (Daniel 2:38).

2. ARMS AND BREAST OF <u>SILVER</u> – MEDO / PERSIA – (Daniel 2:39).

3. HIGHS OF <u>BRONZE</u> – GREECE

4. LEGS OF <u>IRON</u> – ROME

5. FEET OF <u>IRON AND CLAY</u> – DIVIDED KINGDOMS AFTER THE FALL OF ROME.

6. THE GOD WHO GAVE THE DREAM TO NEBUCHADNEZZAR WAS JESUS. HE IS THE ONE COMING BACK TO END THIS WORLD; AND HIS KINGDOM IS AN EVERLASTING ONE.

7. THE GOD WHO REVEALED THE DREAM AND THE MEANING TO DANIEL WAS JESUS WHO IS COMING BACK AS THE ROCK THAT HITS THE IMAGE AT <u>THE FOOT OF IRON AND CLAY</u>.

8. NOTE: THE ROCK REFERS TO THE SECOND COMING OF JESUS – THAT WILL TAKE PLACE DURING THE TIME OF THE DIVIDED KINGDOMS IN EUROPE, AFTER THE FALL OF THE ROMAN EMPIRE IN 476 A.D.

The Dream and the interpretation of Daniel Chapter 2 are certain. God reiterated this fulfillment in Daniel Chapter 7 by <u>another dream</u>. And the dream in Daniel 7 was made by Daniel.

In Daniel 7, God expanded the information in regard to <u>the fourth</u> nation which is Rome where <u>a little horn power</u> emerges out of <u>Rome</u> that is against God's people. This <u>little horn power</u> thinks and attempts to change times and the law of God – (Daniel 7:25). He will persecute the saints of the most-High God which is JESUS. And time is given for him to do exactly, but the saints will prevail and live with God eternally.

CHECK OUT THE HORIZONTAL TIME LINE BELOW THAT SHOWS THE NATIONS FROM THE TIME OF BABYLON AS REVEALED IN THE DREAM TO NEBUCHADNEZZAR IN DANIEL CHAPTER 2.

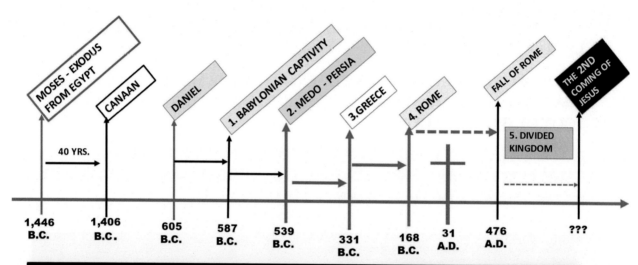

1. THE RETURN OF JESUS WILL TAKE PLACE DURING THE TIME OF THE DIVIDED KINGDOMS, AS PREDICTED IN DANIEL CHAPTER 2 – THE FORGOTTEN DREAM OF KING NEBUCHADNEZZAR OF BABYLON.

2. THE ROCK THAT SMASHES THE IMAGE IN DANIEL CHAPTER 2 REFERS TO THE 2 ND COMING OF JESUS.

May the prophecy in Daniel Chapter 2 give us a boost in understanding that JESUS alone is God, Elohim, Yahweh, Jehovah of Abraham, Isaac, and Jacob.

JESUS is the only one that is coming back. Therefore, there is <u>no</u> Trinity God mentioned in the Bible.

CHAPTER 8

GOD (ELOHIM / YAHWEH / JEHOVAH) INCARNATED INTO HUMAN FLESH

When you come to a clearer understanding about JESUS who was the ELOHIM / YAHWEH / JEHOVAH who created heaven and earth in six days and rested on the Seventh day (Genesis 1:1-31; 2:1-3), you will <u>not</u> believe again in the <u>Trinity God</u> theory <u>nor</u> in the <u>Triune God</u> theory.

Of course, you will <u>not</u> believe that GOD the Father gave birth to a begotten Son called JESUS in heaven because that would contradict JESUS who was the YAHWEH who made heaven and earth. This is commonsense and logic thinking.

YAHWEH (JEHOVAH) became human flesh and was called – JESUS, THE SON OF GOD when He was incarnated and born of Mary at Bethlehem around 04 B.C. . . . Prior to that time, JESUS was <u>not</u> the Son of God in heaven nor in the Old Testament time.

///

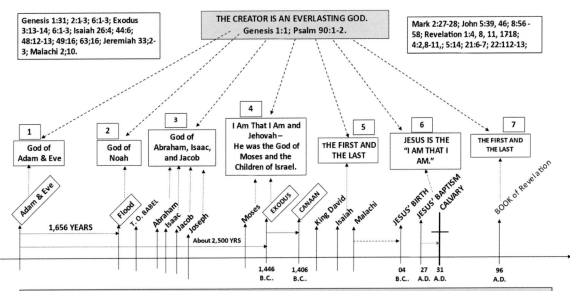

Genesis 1:31; 2:1-3; 6:1-3; Exodus 3:13-14; 6:1-3; Isaiah 26:4; 44:6; 48:12-13; 49:16; 63;16; Jeremiah 33;2-3; Malachi 2;10.

THE CREATOR IS AN EVERLASTING GOD. Genesis 1:1; Psalm 90:1-2.

Mark 2:27-28; John 5:39, 46; 8:56-58; Revelation 1:4, 8, 11, 1718; 4:2,8-11,; 5:14; 21:6-7; 22:112-13;

1 God of Adam & Eve

2 God of Noah

3 God of Abraham, Isaac, and Jacob

4 I Am That I Am and Jehovah – He was the God of Moses and the Children of Israel.

5 THE FIRST AND THE LAST

6 JESUS IS THE "I AM THAT I AM."

7 THE FIRST AND THE LAST

Adam & Eve — 1,656 YEARS — Flood — T. O. BABEL — Abraham, Isaac, Jacob, Joseph — About 2,500 YRS — Moses — EXODUS — CANAAN — King David — Isaiah — Malachi — JESUS' BIRTH — JESUS' BAPTISM — CALVARY — BOOK of Revelation

1,446 B.C. — 1,406 B.C. — 04 B.C. — 27 A.D. — 31 A.D. — 96 A.D.

In the Old Testament, the Jews knew only One God in contrast to the idol gods of the heathen nations. He was the Creator. And He was the Almighty God of Abraham, the Father of the children of Israel. The Jews did NOT know that the Creator, the Almighty God of Abraham would become human flesh through Mary and be born at Bethlehem, and will be called "JESUS," the Son of God. (Luke 1:25; Matthew 1:21-23).

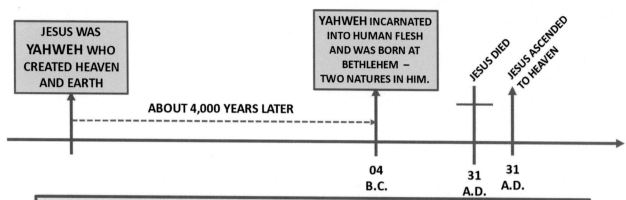

1. Virgin Mary gave birth to the humanity of YAHWEH which is called JESUS, the Son of God – Isaiah 7:14; 9:6; Matthew 1:21- 23; Luke 1:35.

2. Mary did not give birth to YAHWEH'S divinity because God is eternal and cannot be born.

3. At Calvary, only the <u>humanity</u> of YAHWEH died. His divinity did <u>not die; for it cannot</u> die.

4. When JESUS (YAHWEH) ascended to heaven, 40 days after his resurrection, he took his humanity with him.

•

•THE GOD WHO CREATED HEAVEN AND EARTH DID <u>NOT</u> HAVE A BEGOTTEN SON CALLED JESUS IN HEAVEN BEFORE THE ANGELS EXISTED.

• JESUS WAS THE YAHWEH (JEHOVAH) WHO CREATED HEAVEN AND EARTH.

• JESUS IS THE ONLY GOD IN HEAVEN.

• HE IS THE EVERLASTING FATHER WHO BECAME THE SON OF GOD BY INCARNATION THROUGH MARY AT BETHLEHEM.

- • Genesis 1:1-31; 2:1-3; Exodus 3:13,14; 6:1-3; Isaiah 26:4; 43:10; 44:6, 24; 49:16;
- • Matthew 4:4-10; Mark 2:27-28; John 5:39, 46; 8:12; 8:58; Revelation 1:9-11; 17-18; 21:6-7.

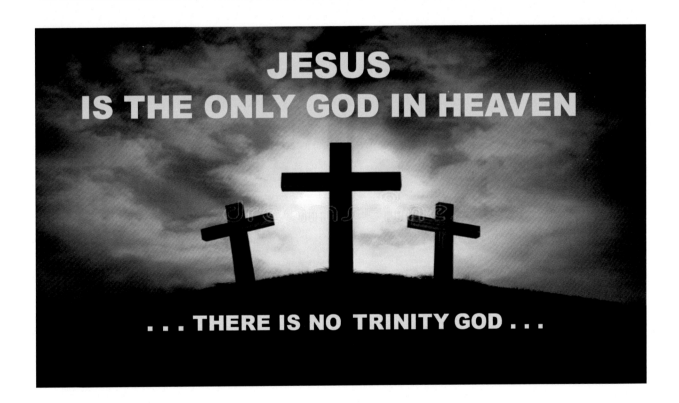

CHAPTER 9

GOD (ELOHIM / YAHWEH / JEHOVAH) GAVE BIRTH TO <u>NO</u> SON IN HEAVEN

JESUS was the Elohim / Yahweh / Jehovah who created heaven and earth in six days and rested on the seventh day. HE was the Almighty God of Abraham who spoke to Moses at the burning bush; and is called – "I AM THAT I AM" – (Exodus 3:13-14; John 8:58).

HE was the God called – the first and the last, who revealed himself to prophet Isaiah.

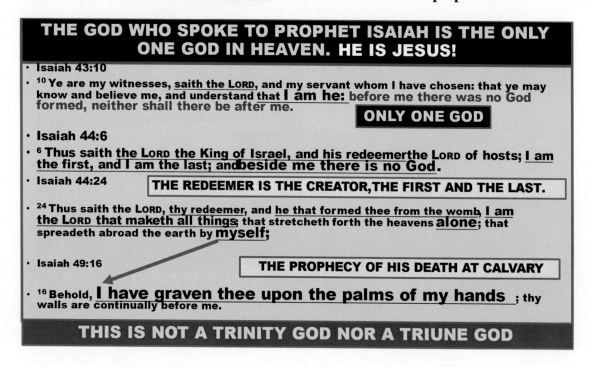

THE GOD WHO SPOKE TO PROPHET ISAIAH IS THE ONLY ONE GOD IN HEAVEN. HE IS JESUS!

- Isaiah 43:10
- [10] Ye are my witnesses, saith the Lord, and my servant whom I have chosen: that ye may know and believe me, and understand that I am he: before me there was no God formed, neither shall there be after me.

ONLY ONE GOD

- Isaiah 44:6
- [6] Thus saith the Lord the King of Israel, and his redeemer the Lord of hosts; I am the first, and I am the last; and beside me there is no God.
- Isaiah 44:24

THE REDEEMER IS THE CREATOR, THE FIRST AND THE LAST.

- [24] Thus saith the Lord, thy redeemer, and he that formed thee from the womb, I am the Lord that maketh all things; that stretcheth forth the heavens alone; that spreadeth abroad the earth by myself;

- Isaiah 49:16

THE PROPHECY OF HIS DEATH AT CALVARY

- [16] Behold, I have graven thee upon the palms of my hands; thy walls are continually before me.

THIS IS NOT A TRINITY GOD NOR A TRIUNE GOD

Therefore, God had <u>no</u> Son called JESUS in heaven before the angels existed.

When Elohim / Yahweh / Jehovah created heaven and earth, He was <u>not</u> called "Jesus" neither "the Son of God" until his birth through Mary at Bethlehem around 04 B.C. - (Matthew 1:21-23; Luke 1:35).

DID YOU NOT KNOW THIS YET? O, yea, God had <u>no</u> Son in heaven at the time when He created heaven and earth and throughout the Old Testament time.

CHAPTER 10

THE MISINTERPRETED TEXT OF THE TRINITY BELIEVERS – GENESIS 1:26

Genesis 1:25-31 (King James Version).

25 And **God** made the beast of the earth after his kind, and cattle after their kind, and every thing that creepeth upon the earth after his kind: and **God** saw that it was good.

26 **And God said, Let us make man in our image, after our likeness**: and let them have dominion over the fish of the sea, and over the fowl of the air, and over the cattle, and over all the earth, and over every creeping thing that creepeth upon the earth.

27 So **God** created man in **his** own image, in the image of **God** created **he** him; male and female created **he** them.

28 And **God** blessed them, and **God** said unto them, Be fruitful, and multiply, and replenish the earth, and subdue it: and have dominion over the fish of the sea, and over the fowl of the air, and over every living thing that moveth upon the earth.

29 And **God** said, Behold, **I** have given you every herb bearing seed, which is upon the face of all the earth, and every tree, in the which is the fruit of a tree yielding seed; to you it shall be for meat.

30 And to every beast of the earth, and to every fowl of the air, and to every thing that creepeth upon the earth, wherein there is life, **I** have given every green herb for meat: and it was so.

31 And God saw every thing that he had made, and, behold, it was very good. And the evening and the morning were the sixth day.

. . . .

- Genesis 1:25-31 King James Version
- 25 And God made the beast of the earth after his kind, and cattle after their kind, and every thing that creepeth upon the earth after his kind: and God saw that it was good.
- 26 And God said, Let us make man in our image, after our likeness: and let them have dominion over the fish of the sea, and over the fowl of the air, and over the cattle, and over all the earth, and over every creeping thing that creepeth upon the earth.
- 27 So God created man in his own image, in the image of God created he him; male and female created he them.
- 28 And God blessed them, and God said unto them, Be fruitful, and multiply, and replenish the earth, and subdue it: and have dominion over the fish of the sea, and over the fowl of the air, and over every living thing that moveth upon the earth.
- 29 And God said, Behold, I have given you every herb bearing seed, which is upon the face of all the earth, and every tree, in the which is the fruit of a tree yielding seed; to you it shall be for meat.
- 30 And to every beast of the earth, and to every fowl of the air, and to every thing that creepeth upon the earth, wherein there is life, I have given every green herb for meat: and it was so.
- 31 And God saw every thing that he had made, and, behold, it was very good. And the evening and the morning were the sixth day.

> **GENESUS 1:5, 10, 16, 27, 29, 31; 2:1-3 =THE PRONOUN IS IN SINGULAR FORM**

. . . .

1. WHAT IS GOD'S IMAGE?

Answer: God is holy. HE is sinless. Therefore, God's image is about sinlessness. All whom God created in His image were sinless beings.

NOTE: God created Adam and Eve as sinless beings. They were made in God's image which is sinless. They were not created in Satan's image which is sinful.

God's image (sinlessness) is the opposite of Satan's image (sinfulness). This is something that most people who claimed to be Christians still have not understood yet, and that is the reason they still believed in these two false doctrines – (1) God created baby sinners from Adam's sin, (2) The Trinity God which is the Triune God.

. . . .

Unfortunately, most people who professed to believe in JESUS as their Creator and Savior, still don't know God's image in Genesis 1:26-27. So sad.

That is the reason they are confused and continued to believe in the TRINITY doctrine because of their misinterpretation of these two Scriptures – Genesis 1:26-27.

After having understood God's image which is sinless, now we are going to ask another question to help us understand Genesis 1:26.

2. WHO ELSE BESIDES GOD HAD GOD'S IMAGE (SINLESS) <u>BEFORE</u> HE MADE ADAM AND EVE IN HIS IMAGE, AS IN GENESIS 1:27?

Answer: The unfallen angels in heaven still has God's image before Adam and Eve were created. The <u>unfallen angels were sinless.</u>

Remember, <u>Lucifer and one third of the angels</u> had fallen and they no longer reflect God's image. They became sinful, <u>not</u> sinless. They had fallen *before* God created Adam and Eve.

NOTE: The next question below should help us clarify the text – Genesis 1:26 and give us a clearer understanding.

3. WHO WAS GOD TALKING TO IN <u>GENESIS 1:26</u> WHO HAD THE SAME IMAGE AS GOD BEFORE HE MADE ADAM AND EVE <u>AS SINLESS BEINGS</u>?

Answer # 1: <u>Possibly</u>, God was talking to the <u>unfallen angels who had God's image</u>.

Answer # 2: <u>Possibly</u>, God was talking to the <u>angel Gabriel</u> who had God's image. He was the angel who came and spoke to Mary about her pregnancy that the baby is to be called – <u>Jesus, the Son of God</u> (Matthew 1:21-23; Luke 1:35).

That proves the point that there was <u>NO Trinity God</u> created Adam and Eve in Genesis 1:26 - 27.

Further proof. Read Genesis 1:29, 31; and 2:1-3 which also proves <u>the singularity of God</u> in the pronouns used. And read the Book of Isaiah where God spoke to the prophet and informed him that there is <u>no</u> God *before* and *after* Him.

. . . .

CHAPTER 11

JOHN ADVOCATED "THE TWO GODS THEORY" WHICH IS WRONG – JOHN 1:1

Scripture – John 1:1.

In the beginning was the Word, and the Word was with God, and the Word was God.

. . . .

EXPLANATION

According to the disciple John, the Word is JESUS who became human flesh (John 1:14), the Son of God, and he is also God distinct from God the Father.

John is promoting a "TWO GOD THEORY" in the Scripture John 1:1.

Most people and Protestant Churches have not seen the error of this text which was the belief of John when he wrote the gospel.

John did not know that JESUS was the everlasting Father of the children of Israel who delivered their forefathers from slavery in Egypt.

John did not know that JESUS was the Almighty God of Abraham, Isaac, and Jacob that he read in the Old Testament.

NOTE: John was correct in declaring JESUS as the Messiah, the Son of God born at Bethlehem through Mary. But was wrong in making Jesus a Son of God born by God the Father in heaven before the angels existed.

John failed to understand that JESUS was the "Elohim" (Yahweh / Jehovah) who created heaven and earth in six days and rested on the seventh day, that you read in the Old Testament – (Genesis 1:1-31; 2:1-3; Exodus 3:13-14; Isaiah 43:10; 44:6, 24; 49:16).

THE TRUTH VERSUS THE ERROR.

IN THE SLIDE BELOW, I PLACED THE TRUTH FROM THE BOOK OF ISAIAH ON THE LEFT SIDE, AND THE SCRIPTURES BY JOHN ON THE RIGHT SIDE, IN ORDER TO HELP YOU AS THE READER TO RECOGNIZE THE ERROR (CONTRADICTION) BY THE DISCIPLE JOHN.

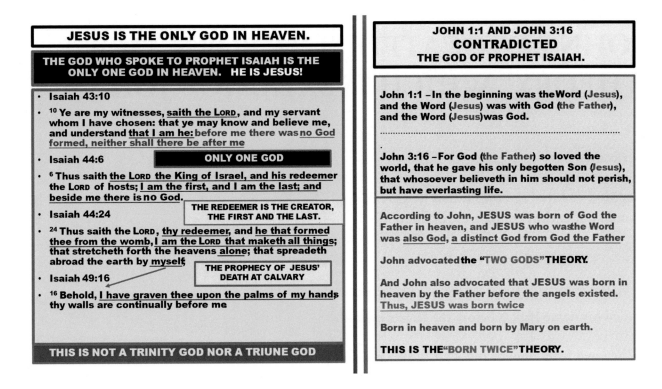

The Powerpoint slide is prepared by Metusela F. Albert.

CHAPTER 12

JOHN ADVOCATED "THE BORN TWICE THEORY" WHICH IS SATANIC – JOHN 3:16

Scripture:

For <u>God</u> so loved the world, that he gave <u>his only begotten Son</u>, that whosoever believeth in him should not perish, but have ever lasting life.

. . . .

TAKE NOTE: According to John 3:16, God the Father gave birth to a begotten Son in heaven, and called his name <u>JESUS</u> before the angels existed.

When you fully understand who JESUS was in the Book of Isaiah, then you would have seen that what John wrote in John 1:1-3, 14 and 3:16 is a contradiction.

THE GOD WHO SPOKE TO PROPHET ISAIAH IS THE ONLY ONE GOD IN HEAVEN. HE IS JESUS!

- Isaiah 43:10
- [10] Ye are my witnesses, <u>saith the LORD</u>, and my servant whom I have chosen: that ye may know and believe me, and understand that <u>I am he:</u> before me there was no God formed, neither shall there be after me.

ONLY ONE GOD

- Isaiah 44:6
- [6] Thus saith the LORD the King of Israel, and his redeemer the LORD of hosts; <u>I am the first, and I am the last; and beside me there is no God</u>.
- Isaiah 44:24

THE REDEEMER IS THE CREATOR, THE FIRST AND THE LAST.

- [24] Thus saith the LORD, thy redeemer, and he that formed thee from the womb, <u>I am the LORD that maketh all things</u>; that stretcheth forth the heavens **alone**; that spreadeth abroad the earth by **myself**;

- Isaiah 49:16

THE PROPHECY OF HIS DEATH AT CALVARY

- [16] Behold, **I have graven thee upon the palms of my hands**; thy walls are continually before me.

THIS IS NOT A TRINITY GOD NOR A TRIUNE GOD

This truth will come as a shock to many professed Christians and Pastors who have been believing in what John wrote in John 1:1-3, and 3:16 for so many years.

That is also a contradiction to Revelation 4:1-11, the only God who is sitting on the Throne in heaven which is JESUS. Read Chapter 13 of this book.

Are you still not convinced yet? Well, read *the first* commandment of the Ten Commandments in Exodus 20:1-3.

What John wrote in John 1:1-3 and 3:16 contradicted Exodus 20:1-3.

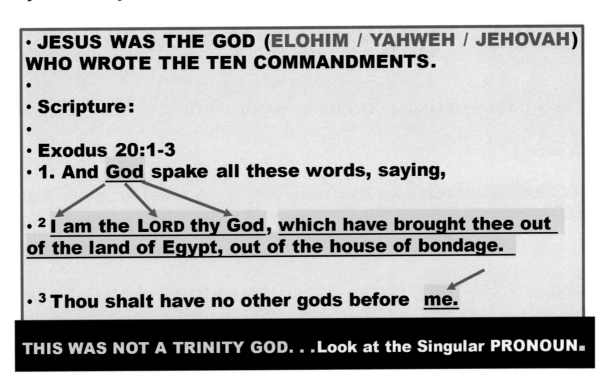

• **JESUS WAS THE GOD (ELOHIM / YAHWEH / JEHOVAH) WHO WROTE THE TEN COMMANDMENTS.**
•
• **Scripture:**
•
• **Exodus 20:1-3**
• **1. And God spake all these words, saying,**

• **2 I am the LORD thy God, which have brought thee out of the land of Egypt, out of the house of bondage.**

• **3 Thou shalt have no other gods before me.**

THIS WAS NOT A TRINITY GOD. . .Look at the Singular PRONOUN.

John was correct in believing that Jesus was the Messiah, the Son of God, that was born of Mary at Bethlehem. That is not the issue in here.

But John was wrong in advocating that Jesus was born by God the Father in heaven before his incarnation through Mary at Bethlehem. This is the BORN TWICE theory by John.

Unfortunately, most PROTESTANT CHURCHES are believing in the "BORN TWICE THEORY" because they believed what John wrote in John 1:1 and 3:16.

CHAPTER 13

PAUL ADVOCATED "<u>THE BORN TWICE THEORY</u>" ALSO WHICH IS SATANIC

PAUL SAYS, JESUS IS SITTING ON THE RIGHT HAND OF GOD THE FATHER IN HEAVEN.

Romans 8:11

[11] But if **<u>the Spirit of him that raised up Jesus</u>** from the dead dwell in you, **<u>he that raised up Christ from the dead</u>** shall also quicken your mortal bodies by his Spirit that dwelleth in you.

//

Romans 8:32-34 = JESUS IS SITTING ON THE RIGHT HAND OF GOD.

[32] **<u>He that spared not his own Son</u>**, but delivered him up for us all, how shall he not with him also freely give us all things?

[33] Who shall lay any thing to the charge of God's elect? It is <u>God</u> that justifieth.

[34] Who is he that condemneth? It is Christ that died, yea rather, that is risen again, <u>who is even at the right hand of God, who also maketh intercession for us</u>.

//

1 Corinthians 1:9

[9] <u>God is faithful</u>, by whom ye were called unto the fellowship of <u>his Son Jesus Christ our Lord.</u>

//

1 Corinthians 8:6

⁶ But to us there is but <u>one God</u>, <u>the Father</u>, of whom are all things, and we in him; and <u>one Lord Jesus Christ</u>, by whom are all things, and we by him.

//

1 Corinthians 11:3

³ But I would have you know, that the head of every man is Christ; and the head of the woman is the man; and <u>the head of Christ is God</u>.

//

GALATIANS 1:3 - 4

³ Grace be to you and peace from <u>God the Father</u>, and from <u>our Lord Jesus Christ</u>,

⁴ Who gave himself for our sins, that he might deliver us from this present evil world, according to <u>the will of God and our Father</u>:

. . . .

COLOSSIANS 1:2-3

² To the saints and faithful brethren in Christ which are at Colosse: Grace be unto you, and peace, <u>from God our Father and the Lord Jesus Christ</u>.

³ We give thanks <u>to God and the Father of our Lord Jesus Christ</u>, praying always for you,

. . . .

1 Timothy 2:5 - King James Version

⁵ For there <u>is one God</u>, and <u>one mediator between God and men</u>, the <u>man Christ Jesus</u>;

. . . .

COLOSSIANS 1:12-20

¹² Giving thanks unto <u>the Father</u>, which hath made us meet to be partakers of the inheritance of the saints in light:

¹³ Who hath delivered us from the power of darkness, and hath translated us into the kingdom of <u>his dear Son</u>:

¹⁴ In whom we have redemption through his blood, even the forgiveness of sins:

¹⁵ <u>Who is the image of the invisible God, the firstborn of every creature</u>:

¹⁶ For by <u>him were all things created</u>, that are in heaven, and that are in earth, visible and invisible, whether they be thrones, or dominions, or principalities, or powers: <u>all things were created by him, and for him</u>:

¹⁷ And he is before all things, and by him all things consist.

¹⁸ And he is the head of the body, the church: who is the beginning, <u>the firstborn from the dead</u>; that in all things he might have the preeminence.

¹⁹ For it pleased <u>the Father</u> that in him should all fulness dwell;

²⁰ And, having made peace through the blood of his cross, by him to reconcile all things unto himself; by him, I say, whether they be things in earth, or things in heaven.

//

REVELATION 4:1-11

4 After this I looked, and, behold, a door was opened in heaven: and the first voice which I heard was as it were of a trumpet talking with me; which said, Come up hither, and I will shew thee things which must be hereafter.

² And immediately I was in the spirit: and, <u>behold, a throne was set in heaven</u>, <u>and one sat on the throne.</u>

³ And he that sat was to look upon like a jasper and a sardine stone: and there was a rainbow round about the throne, in sight like unto an emerald.

⁴ And round about the throne were four and twenty seats: and upon the seats I saw four and twenty elders sitting, clothed in white raiment; and they had on their heads crowns of gold.

⁵ And out of the throne proceeded lightnings and thunderings and voices: and there were seven lamps of fire burning before the throne, which are the seven Spirits of God.

⁶ And before the throne there was a sea of glass like unto crystal: and in the midst of the throne, and round about the throne, were four beasts full of eyes before and behind.

⁷ And the first beast was like a lion, and the second beast like a calf, and the third beast had a face as a man, and the fourth beast was like a flying eagle.

⁸ And the four beasts had each of them six wings about him; and they were full of eyes within: and

they rest not day and night, saying, Holy, holy, holy, LORD God Almighty, which was, and is, and is to come.

⁹ And when those beasts give glory and honour and thanks to him that sat on the throne, who liveth for ever and ever,

¹⁰ The four and twenty elders fall down before him that sat on the throne, and worship him that liveth for ever and ever, and cast their crowns before the throne, saying,

. . . .

When Paul died around 66-68 A.D., he had written about 14 letters to the Churches in minor Asia. He was correct in believing and expressing that JESUS whom the Jews killed at Calvary was the Messiah, the Savior of mankind.

Paul wrote that the Father is God, and JESUS is the visible Son of God who came from heaven. According to Paul, the Father and JESUS were two distinct beings.

When Paul mentioned God the Father in his letters, he was referring to a distinct person who was the Almighty God of Abraham who is the only one God in heaven.

Paul did not really understand that the Almighty God of Abraham was JESUS who later became incarnated into human flesh at Bethlehem through Mary.

. . . .

THE TRUTH IS:

- It was not the Son of God who became human flesh at Bethlehem through Mary.

- It was YAHWEH, JEHOVAH who became the Son of God in human flesh at Bethlehem through Mary, and is called - JESUS.

. . . .

CHAPTER 14

JESUS IS THE <u>ONLY GOD</u> SITTING ON THE THRONE IN HEAVEN – REVELATION 4

Worship is due to him as the Creator.

Let's Read Revelation 4:1-11 – (King James Version).

1. After this I looked, and, behold, a door was opened in heaven: and the first voice which I

heard was as it were of a trumpet talking with me; which said, Come up hither, and I will shew thee things which must be hereafter.

² And immediately I was in the spirit: and, behold, <u>a throne was set in heaven, and one sat on the throne.</u>

³ And <u>he that sat was to look upon like a jasper and a sardine stone: and there was a rainbow round about the throne, in sight like unto an emerald.</u>

⁴ And round about the throne were four and twenty seats: and upon the seats I saw four and twenty elders sitting, clothed in white raiment; and they had on their heads crowns of gold.

⁵ And out of the throne proceeded lightnings and thunderings and voices: and there were seven lamps of fire burning before the throne, which are the seven Spirits of God.

⁶ And before the throne there was a sea of glass like unto crystal: and in the midst of the throne, and round about the throne, were four beasts full of eyes before and behind.

⁷ And the first beast was like a lion, and the second beast like a calf, and the third beast had a face as a man, and the fourth beast was like a flying eagle.

⁸ And the four beasts had each of them six wings about him; and they were full of eyes within: and

they rest not day and night, saying, <u>Holy, holy, holy, L</u>ORD <u>God Almighty, which was, and is, and is to come.</u>

⁹ And when <u>those beasts give glory and honour and thanks to him that sat on the throne, who liveth for ever and ever,</u>

¹⁰ The four and twenty elders <u>fall down before him that sat on the throne, and worship him that liveth for ever and ever</u>, and cast their crowns before the throne, saying,

¹¹ <u>Thou art worthy, O Lord, to receive glory and honour and power: for thou hast created all things, and for thy pleasure they are and were created</u>.

. . . .

SUMMARY

Four important points mentioned in Revelation Chapter 4 about the one on the Throne.

1. Only <u>one God</u> sat on the throne (v2).

2. He was the LORD GOD ALMIGHTY, which was, is, and is to come (v8).

3. Worship is due to the one on the throne. he that <u>liveth for ever and ever</u> (v10).

4. He <u>created all things</u> (v11).

JESUS IS THE ONLY <u>ONE</u> THAT FITS INTO THOSE FOUR POINTS MENTIONED IN REVELATION CHAPTER 4.

Jesus, the first and the last; he who created heaven and earth became human flesh, died, resurrected, and lived for ever and ever.

Isaiah 43:10; 44:6, 24; 49:16; Revelation 1:17-18; 21:6-7.

///

JESUS WAS THE CREATOR (YAHWEH / JEHOVAH) WHO BECAME THE GOD OF ABRAHAM, ISAAC, AND JACOB.

JESUS IS THE ONE SITTING ON THE THRONE IN HEAVEN.

Worship is due to the Creator – Exodus 3:13-14; 6:1-3; 20:1-3; Matthew 4:7-10; John 8:56-58; Revelation 4:1-11; 14:6-7.

JESUS BECAME THE LAMB THAT WAS SLAIN FROM THE FOUNDATION OF THE EARTH – Revelation 13:8, John 1:29.

JESUS was dead and alive forever more. HE ascended to heaven and took His human flesh with Him. His hands and legs with the nail prints can be seen in His resurrected body.

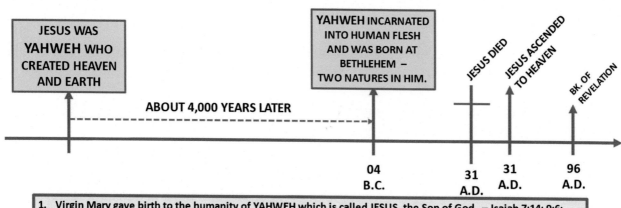

1. Virgin Mary gave birth to the humanity of YAHWEH which is called JESUS, the Son of God – Isaiah 7:14; 9:6; Matthew 1:21- 23; Luke 1:35.

2. Mary did not give birth to YAHWEH'S divinity because God is eternal and cannot be born.

3. At Calvary, only the humanity of YAHWEH died. His divinity did not die; for it cannot die.

4. When JESUS (YAHWEH) ascended to heaven, 40 days after his resurrection, he took his humanity with him.

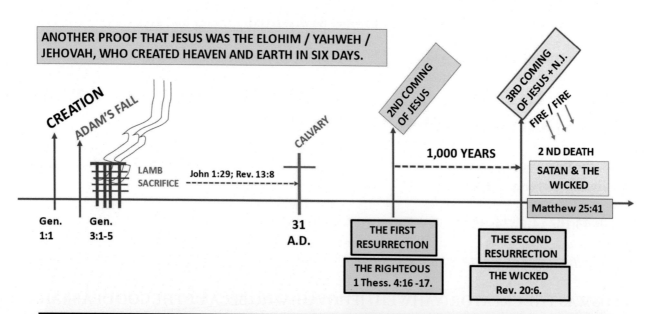

ANOTHER PROOF THAT JESUS WAS THE ELOHIM / YAHWEH / JEHOVAH, WHO CREATED HEAVEN AND EARTH IN SIX DAYS.

JESUS IS "THE GOD" WHO IS COMING BACK WITH THE BREATH OF LIFE TO GIVE LIFE TO THE RIGHTEOUS DEAD TO RESURRECT IN THE FIRST RESURRECTION.

•

•THE GOD OF ABRAHAM, ISAAC, AND JACOB CALLED – "I AM THAT I AM," HE IS JESUS.

• JESUS IS THE <u>ONLY</u> GOD IN HEAVEN.

• HE IS THE <u>EVERLASTING</u> <u>FATHER</u> WHO BECAME THE SON OF GOD BY INCARNATION THROUGH MARY AT BETHLEHEM.

- **Genesis 1:1-31; 2:1-3; Exodus 3:13,14; 6:1-3; Isaiah 26:4; 43:10; 44:6, 24; 49:16;**
- **Matthew 4:410; Mark 2:27-28; John 5:39, 46; 8:12; 8:58; Revelation 1:9-11; 17-18; 21:6-7.**

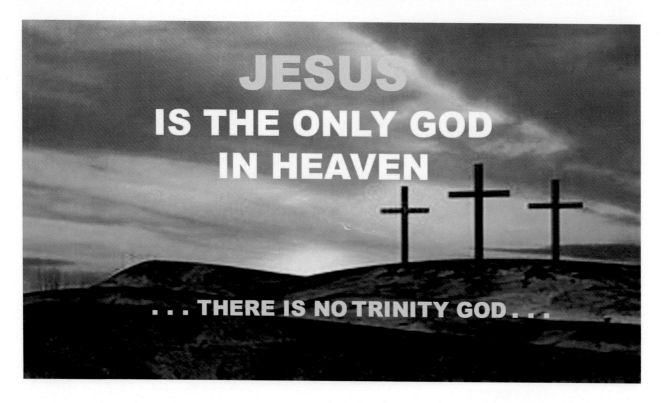

Revelation chapter 4 cannot contradict Revelation chapter 5 and the book of Isaiah.

CHAPTER 15

JESUS, <u>AS A HUMAN BEING</u>, WAS THE LAMB SLAIN – REVELATION 5

Let's read Revelation 5:1-14 – (King James Version).

1. And I saw in <u>the right hand of him that sat on the throne a book written within and on the backside, sealed with seven seals</u>.

² And I saw a strong angel proclaiming with a loud voice, Who is worthy to open the book, and to loose the seals thereof?

³ And no man in heaven, nor in earth, neither under the earth, was able to open the book, neither to look thereon.

⁴ And I wept much, <u>because no man</u> was found worthy to open and to read the book, neither to look thereon.

⁵ And one of the elders saith unto me, <u>Weep not: behold, the Lion of the tribe of Judah, the Root of David, hath prevailed to open the book, and to loose the seven seals thereof.</u>

⁶ And I beheld, and, lo, in the midst of the throne and of the four beasts, and in the midst of the elders, <u>stood a Lamb as it had been slain</u>, having seven horns and seven eyes, which are the seven Spirits of God sent forth into all the earth.

⁷ And <u>he came and took the book out of the right hand of him that sat upon the throne</u>.

⁸ And when he had taken the book, the four beasts and four and twenty elders fell down before the Lamb, having every one of them harps, and golden vials full of odours, which are the prayers of saints.

⁹ And they sung a new song, saying, <u>Thou art worthy to take the book, and to open the seals thereof: for thou wast slain, and hast redeemed us to God by thy blood out of every kindred, and tongue, and people, and nation;</u>

¹⁰ And hast made us unto our God kings and priests: and we shall reign on the earth.

¹¹ And I beheld, and I heard the voice of many angels round about the throne and the beasts and the elders: and the number of them was ten thousand times ten thousand, and thousands of thousands;

¹² Saying with a loud voice, <u>Worthy is the Lamb that was slain to receive power, and riches, and wisdom, and strength, and honour, and glory, and blessing</u>.

¹³ And every creature which is in heaven, and on the earth, and under the earth, and such as are in the sea, and all that are in them, heard I saying, Blessing, and honour, and glory, and power, <u>be unto him that sitteth upon the throne, and unto the Lamb for ever and ever</u>.

¹⁴ And the four beasts said, Amen. And the four and twenty elders fell down and <u>worshipped him that liveth for ever and ever</u>.

. . . .

EXPLANATION

1. There is only <mark>one GOD</mark> that sits on the THRONE.

2. He is alive for ever and ever.

3. The four beasts and twenty-four elders worship Him on the Throne.

4. The <u>lamb that was slain</u> is the only one who is able to take the book from the right hand of the one sitting on the Throne.

. . . .

The lamb that was slain is JESUS <u>in humanity</u>. HE is the Son. That is the only one who can take the book from the one sitting on the Throne, and open it.

The one sitting on the Throne is JESUS, <u>the Father in divinity</u>. HE alone was dead and alive forever more.

. . . .

The vision given to John on the Island of Patmos for him to write the prophetic Book called "REVELATION", is for him to understand that JESUS whom he knew as the Son of Mary who died at Calvary, <u>is also the Father, the only God who is sitting on the Throne</u>.

When John wrote his gospel, he did <u>not</u> understand who JESUS really was in the Old Testament time. But the Book of Revelation is a revelation from JESUS to John on the ISLAND OF PATMOS. In the Book of Revelation, JESUS revealed himself as the Alpha and Omega, the First and the Last who spoke to prophet Isaiah in the Old Testament.

Even Paul did <u>not</u> know that JESUS was the Almighty God of Abraham when he wrote his 14 letters to the Churches. Of course, Paul knew JESUS as the Messiah on the road to Damascus, <u>but not</u> as God the Father, the Almighty God of Abraham, Isaac, and Jacob who wrote the Ten Commandments.

HERE IS SOMETHING TO THINK – Most Protestant Churches today still have not understood yet that JESUS was the Almighty God of Abraham, the only God in heaven.

JESUS WHO WAS YAHWEH (JEHOVAH) IS THE ONLY GOD SITTING ON THE THRONE IN HEAVEN.

JESUS, AS A HUMAN BEING, WAS THE LAMB SLAIN FROM THE FOUNDATION OF THE EARTH WHO CAN TAKE THE BOOK FROM THE ONE SITTING ON THE THRONE.

Revelation Chapters 4 and 5, points to one Divine Being, and He is JESUS.

NOTE: Revelation chapters 4 and 5 are talking of JESUS as the only God sitting on the Throne. And JESUS, <u>as a human being</u>, was the lamb slain from the foundation of the earth. He alone is the <u>only man</u> who can take the book from the right hand of God. JESUS is God also. HE alone is God. There is no other God *before* and *after* him.

Keep in mind, there was only one God who spoke to prophet Isaiah in the Old Testament – (Isaiah 43:10; 44:6, 24; 49:16). Therefore, there is <u>no</u> Trinity God.

FURTHER READING - Revelation 1:9-11; 17:18; 13:8; 21:6-7; 22:18-19; 1 John 1:29.

CHAPTER 16

WHILE IN HUMAN FLESH, JESUS HAD <u>TWO NATURES</u> (HUMAN AND DIVINE)

Prior to the incarnation at Bethlehem through Mary, JESUS was the YAHWEH (JEHOVAH) who created heaven and earth in six days (Genesis 1:1-31; 2:1-3). He who created heaven and earth was <u>fully divine</u>. HE was <u>an eternal God</u>; <u>not</u> a Son of God. There was <u>no</u> Son of God in heaven before the incarnation at Bethlehem.

When YAHWEH (JEHOVAH) took upon himself human flesh by the incarnation process through Mary at Bethlehem, he did <u>not</u> cease from being the everlasting God who created heaven and earth.

Therefore, JESUS had <u>the divine nature</u> and <u>the human nature</u> while in human flesh. Both natures, the divinity and humanity were in one person.

JESUS was the everlasting Father in the Old Testament who became the Son of God in the New Testament at Bethlehem through Mary.

It was only <u>the humanity</u> of JESUS that was born of Mary at Bethlehem because his divinity cannot be born.

Let's be very clear. Mary was <u>not</u> the mother of God. She was <u>not</u> the mother of the divinity of JESUS.

It was only <u>the humanity of JESUS that died at Calvary</u> because his divinity cannot die. As a divine being, he was <u>immortal</u>. But as a human being like us, he was <u>mortal</u> and that is why the Romans were able to kill him at Calvary. The Romans did not kill God. Nobody can kill God.

JESUS, as the everlasting God, the resurrection and the life, He resurrected his human body from the grave. Remember, he said, <u>"Destroy this temple, and in three days I will raise it up"</u> – (John 2:19).

As a human being like us, <u>JESUS</u> did <u>not</u> have the power to perform miracles. But as an everlasting God, He was able to perform the miracles – feeding over 5,000 people out of five loaves and two fishes, raising the dead like Lazarus, healing the sick, etc.

As God, JESUS had the power to resurrect Lazarus from the grave – (John 11:25). As God, JESUS had the right to forgive sins – (Mark 2:1-10). He not only forgave the sins of the paralytic, but healed the paralytic completely.

JESUS AS GOD, KNOWS THE DAY AND HOUR OF HIS RETURN.

<u>As God</u>, JESUS knows the future, the day and hour of his coming. Of course, He gave us the signs of His return in Matthew 24, which tells us that He knows the day and hour of His coming back. It is obvious.

JESUS who is Alpha and Omega, knew that Judas was going to put his hand in the cup at the last Supper on Thursday evening before His crucifixion on <u>Friday afternoon</u>, the 14th day of Nisan – (Read John Chapters 13 and 14).

JESUS is an everlasting (eternal) God. HE is omnipotent, omniscient, and omnipresent.

. . . .

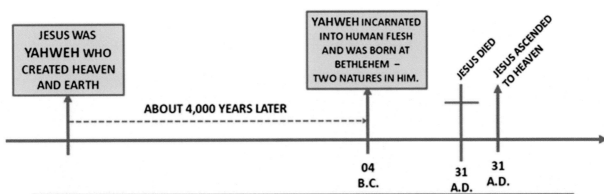

1. Virgin Mary gave birth to the humanity of YAHWEH which is called JESUS, the Son of God – Isaiah 7:14; 9:6; Matthew 1:21- 23; Luke 1:35.

2. Mary did not give birth to YAHWEH'S divinity because God is eternal and cannot be born.

3. At Calvary, only the <u>humanity</u> of YAHWEH died. His divinity did <u>not die; for it cannot</u> die.

4. When JESUS (YAHWEH) ascended to heaven, 40 days after his resurrection, he took his humanity with him.

. . . .

DIAGRAM # 1 - THE TWO NATURES OF JESUS WHILE IN HUMAN FLESH.

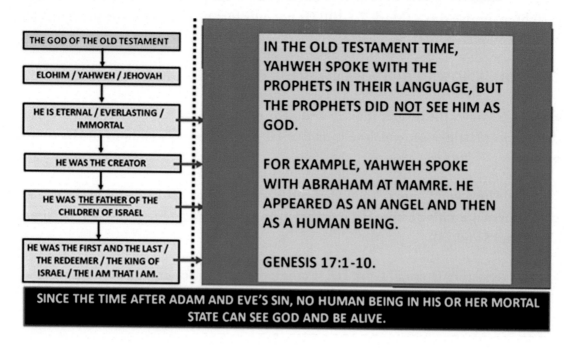

DIAGRAM # 2 – THE TWO NATURES OF JESUS WHILE IN HUMAN FLESH.

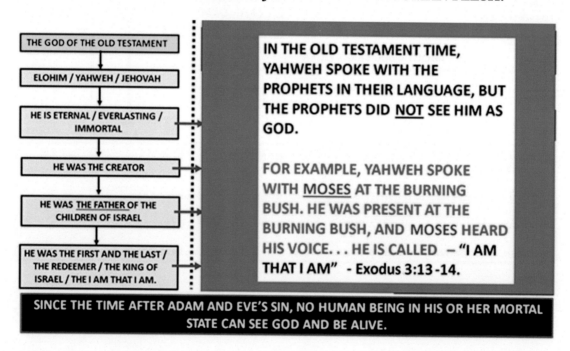

DIAGRAM # 3 – THE TWO NATURES OF JESUS WHILE IN HUMAN FLESH

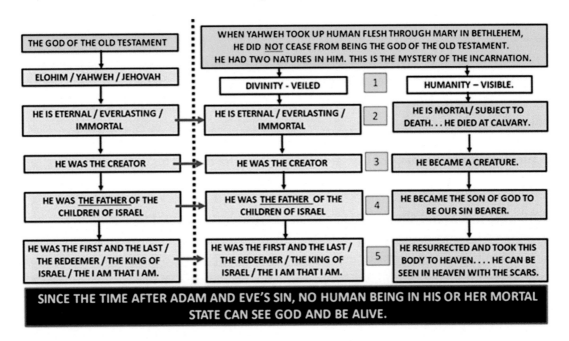

NOTE: If you did <u>not</u> understand who JESUS was in the Old Testament AND the <u>TWO NATURES</u> of JESUS while He was in human flesh, you then will <u>not</u> fully understand many of the sayings He said about himself in the New Testament.

Remember, the disciples and the Jewish leaders did not understand who JESUS was in the Old Testament. And that is why they did not understand the many simple sayings of JESUS about himself. That led the Jewish Church leaders to their rejection and crucifixion of JESUS.

These are some of the simple sayings of Jesus about himself.

1. JESUS said - Before Abraham was, I AM - (John 8:58).

2. JESUS said – Search ye the Scriptures; for in them ye think ye have eternal life; but they are they which testify of me – (John 5:39).

3. JESUS said - Had you believed Moses, you would have believed me; for he wrote about me - (John 5:46).

4. JESUS said – I am the Resurrection and the Life;

5. JESUS said - Nobody comes to the Father but through Me.

6. JESUS said – I and the Father are one.

7. JESUS said - Father, forgive them, for they know not what they do.

8. JESUS taught the disciples to pray, <u>Our Father which art in heaven</u> . . . (Matthew 6).

ANOTHER CLASSICAL EXAMPLE OF JESUS CHRIST'S TWO NATURES

When you come to a better understanding of the incarnation process that GOD (YAHWEH / JEHOVAH) took and became human flesh like us, that should enable you to understand the <u>Two Natures</u> within Himself. That should also help you to understand <u>the sayings of JESUS</u> in the New Testament.

For example, let's look at what JESUS said to Mary on the day of his resurrection, as recorded in John 20:17.

¹⁶ Jesus saith unto her, Mary. She turned herself, and saith unto him, Rabboni; which is to say, Master.

<u>¹⁷ Jesus saith unto her, Touch me not; for I am not yet ascended to my Father: but go to my brethren, and say unto them, I ascend unto my Father, and your Father; and to my God, and your God.</u>

. . . .

. . . .

Even though JESUS is GOD, but he did <u>not</u> use his divine power to benefit himself or to supply his own human needs. When he is hungry or thirsty, he could have supplied his needs by turning the stones into bread or water. At numerous times, JESUS used his divine power <u>to prove his divinity to the unbelieving Jews</u>. For example, the feeding of the five thousand people with five loaves and two fishes; the resurrection of Lazarus from the grave, the healing of the sick, etc.

. . . .

CHAPTER 17

JESUS WAS THE <u>EVERLASTING FATHER</u> IN THE OLD AND NEW TESTAMENTS

There are four simple Scriptures shared below that will prove that JESUS himself was the Everlasting Father of the <u>Old and New</u> Testaments.

. . . .

SCRIPTURE # 1 - Isaiah 7:14 - King James Version

[14] Therefore <u>the Lord himself shall give you a sign</u>; <u>Behold, a virgin shall conceive, and bear a son,</u> and <u>shall call his name</u> <u>Immanuel</u>.

. . . .

SCRIPTURE # 2 - Isaiah 9:6 - King James Version

[6] For unto us <u>a child is born</u>, unto us a son is given: and the government shall be upon his shoulder: and <u>his name shall be called</u> <u>Wonderful, Counsellor, The mighty God, The everlasting Father, The Prince of Peace</u>.

. . . .

SCRIPTURE # 3 - Matthew 1:21-23 - King James Version

[21] And <u>she shall bring forth a son, and thou shalt call his name Jesus</u>: for he shall save his people from their sins.

[22] Now all this was done, that it might be fulfilled which was <u>spoken of the Lord by the prophet</u>, saying,

[23] Behold, <u>a virgin shall be with child</u>, and <u>shall bring forth a son</u>, and they shall call his name <u>Emmanuel</u>, <u>which being interpreted is, God with us</u>.

. . . .

The Book of Isaiah is a prophecy about GOD himself becoming human flesh through a virgin woman. Actually, the virgin woman's name was <u>not</u> given in the Old Testament. However, the birth place of the Messiah was mentioned to be Bethlehem – Micah 5:2.

This <u>child</u> is the Mighty God, the everlasting Father, the Prince of Peace, Immanuel. JESUS is being predicted in the Book of Isaiah to be this child. We read the fulfillment in the Book of Matthew 1:21-23 when JESUS was born of Mary at Bethlehem.

We also see the prophecy about JESUS CHRIST'S death in Isaiah 49:16 and 53:1-10 after the Jews killed him at Calvary.

. . . .

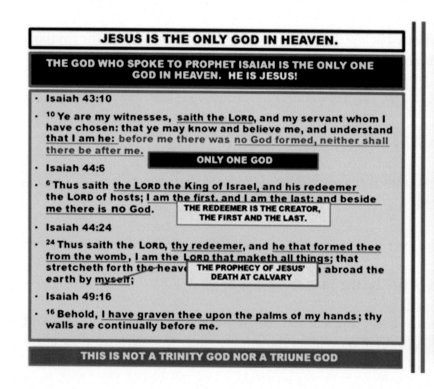

. . . .

DID JESUS DECLARE HIMSELF AS GOD THE FATHER?

Answer: Yes.

SCRIPTURE # 4 - John 14:6-9 - King James Version

⁶ Jesus saith unto him, I am the way, the truth, and the life: no man cometh unto the Father, but by me.

⁷ <u>If ye had known me, ye should have known my Father also: and from henceforth ye know him, and have seen him</u>.

⁸ Philip saith unto him, Lord, show us the Father, and it sufficeth us.

⁹ Jesus saith unto him, <u>Have I been so long time with you, and yet hast thou not known me, Philip? he that hath seen me hath seen the Father; and how sayest thou then, Show us the Father?</u>

. . . .

When the disciples speak of the Father, they are referring to the Almighty God of Abraham, Isaac, and Jacob in the Old Testament. They did <u>not</u> realize that JESUS who was born of Mary at Bethlehem whom they believed to be the Messiah was the Almighty God of Abraham, Isaac, and Jacob in the Old Testament.

Therefore, JESUS in his conversation with Phillip in John 14:6-9, declared that <u>he is the Father</u>.

IF the disciples had read the Old Testament Prophecies in the Book of Isaiah, and believed in what the angel said to Mary about Jesus, they would have believed in him as the Elohim / Yahweh / Jehovah called "I AM THAT I AM" who spoke to Moses at the burning bush.

Therefore, they would have believed what JESUS said of himself, "Before Abraham was, I AM." (John 8:58). And they would have had no problem in believing him as the everlasting Father of the Prophets in the Old Testament when he said, "Had you believed Moses, you would have believed <u>me</u>; for he wrote about <u>me</u>." (John 5:46).

About 2,000 years ago, the disciples did <u>not</u> understand who JESUS was in the Old Testament. Back then, they did not have the New Testament, but they had him in their midst in human flesh. They failed to understand the Book of Isaiah and the prophecies about JESUS.

DON'T MISS THE POINT. The disciples and Paul understood and JESUS as the Messiah, <u>but not</u> as YAHWEH (JEHOVAH) who created heaven and earth who became the God of Abraham, Isaac, and Jacob.

(This is a huge point that most Protestant Churches, Pastors, and Mega Churches including the SDA Church, has not understood yet which caused them to continue to believe in the Trinity doctrine which is the Triune God theory).

. . . .

Today, we have the Old and New Testaments, yet most Churches and mainline denominations still don't know yet that JESUS was the everlasting Father in the Old and New Testaments.

Since JESUS is the only God in heaven, therefore, he alone is the everlasting Father in heaven who humbly became the Son of God by incarnation through Mary at Bethlehem to die at Calvary, as our Sin Bearer.

While in human flesh, JESUS was the everlasting Father as well as the Son of God. HE did not cease from being God the Father when He humbly became the Son of God through Mary at Bethlehem.

JESUS IS THE EVERLASTING FATHER IN HEAVEN. HE IS THE ONLY GOD IN HEAVEN. THERE IS NO OTHER GOD BEFORE AND AFTER HIM.

JESUS IS THE EVERLASTING FATHER

- SCRIPTURE # 1 - Isaiah 7:14 - King James Version

- ¹⁴ Therefore the Lord himself shall give you a sign; Behold, a virgin shall conceive, and bear a son, and shall call his name Immanuel

- SCRIPTURE # 2 - Isaiah 9:6 - King James Version

- ⁶ For unto us a child is born, unto us a son is given: and the government shall be upon his shoulder: and his name shall be called Wonderful, Counsellor, The mighty God, The everlasting Father, The Prince of Peace

- SCRIPTURE # 3 - Matthew 1:21-23 - King James Version

- ²¹ And she shall bring forth a son, and thou shalt call his name JESUS: for he shall save his people from their sins.
- ²² Now all this was done, that it might be fulfilled which was spoken of the Lord by the prophet, saying, ²³ Behold, a virgin shall be with child, and shall bring forth a son, and they shall call his name Emmanuel, which being interpreted, God with us. SCRIPTURE # 4 - John 14:6-9 - King James Version

- ⁶ Jesus saith unto him, I am the way, the truth, and the life: no man cometh unto the Father, but by me.
- ⁷ If ye had known me, ye should have known my Father also: and from henceforth ye know him, and have seen him. ⁸ Philip saith unto him, Lord, show us the Father, and it sufficeth us. ⁹ Jesus saith unto him, Have I been so long time with you, and yet hast thou not known me, Philip? he that hath seen me hath seen the Father; and how sayest thou then, Show us the Father?

JESUS IS THE EVERLASTING FATHER

- SCRIPTURE # 4 - John 14:6-9 - King James Version
- 6 Jesus saith unto him, I am the way, the truth, and the life: no man cometh unto the Father, but by me.
- 7 If ye had known me, ye should have known my Father also: and from henceforth ye know him, and have seen him. 8 Philip saith unto him, Lord, show us the Father, and it sufficeth us. 9 Jesus saith unto him, Have I been so long time with you, and yet hast thou not known me, Philip? he that hath seen me hath seen the Father; and how sayest thou then, Show us the Father?

....

- When the disciples speak of the Father, they are referring to the Almighty God of Abraham, Isaac, and Jacob in the Old Testament. They did not realize that JESUS who was born of Mary at Bethlehem whom they believed to be the Messiah was the Almighty God of Abraham, Isaac, and Jacob in the Old Testament.
-
- Therefore, JESUS in his conversation with Phillip in John 14:6-9, declared that he is the Father.

JESUS WAS THE YAHWEH / JEHOVAH WHO WROTE THE TEN COMMANDMENTS.

- JESUS WAS THE GOD (ELOHIM / YAHWEH / JEHOVAH) WHO WROTE THE TEN COMMANDMENTS.
-
- Scripture:
-
- Exodus 20:1-3
- 1. And God spake all these words, saying,

- 2 I am the LORD thy God, which have brought thee out of the land of Egypt, out of the house of bondage.

- 3 Thou shalt have no other gods before me.

THIS WAS NOT A TRINITY GOD. . .Look at the Singular PRONOUN.

CHAPTER 18

WHO IS THE HOLY SPIRIT?

Listed below are <u>FOUR Scriptures</u> that need explanation to ensure that we understand <u>JESUS as the only one God in heaven.</u> Which means, there is <u>no such thing</u> as three distinct persons existed in heaven.

. . . .

BELOW IS A CRUCIAL POINT THAT NEEDS TO BE UNDERSTOOD BY THE READER OR PASTOR OR EVANGELIST, ETC.

There is <u>only one person</u> (Elohim / Yahweh / Jehovah) who existed in heaven. And that <u>one person</u> is the Father who is also the Holy Spirit and is also <u>the Son by incarnation at Bethlehem through Mary</u>.

. . . .

The Holy Spirit is the Spirit of God – (Genesis 1:2).

The Father (Elohim / Yahweh / Jehovah) took human flesh by incarnation at Bethlehem through Mary, and <u>became the Son of God which is called – JESUS.</u> (Luke 1:35).

The Holy Spirit is the Spirit of JESUS. In other words, Elohim / Yahweh / Jehovah is the Holy Spirit. Therefore, Jesus who is Elohim / Yahweh / Jehovah is the Holy Spirit.

. . . .

NOTE: The belief that says, "God the Father, God the Son, and God the Holy Spirit are <u>three distinct beings,</u> <u>but they act as one God,</u>" is a False teaching.

That is the reason this book is written to help professed Christians turn away from such beliefs that contradicted the truth about JESUS who is the only one God in heaven.

. . . .

1. MATTHEW 3:16-17

2. JOHN 14:16

3. 1 JOHN 5:7

4. Matthew 28:19-20.

. . . .

THE HOLY SPIRIT IS <u>THE SPIRIT OF JESUS</u>.

JOHN 20:19-22

¹⁹ Then the same day at evening, being <u>the first day of the week</u>, when the doors were shut where the disciples were assembled for fear of the Jews, <u>came Jesus and stood in their midst and said unto them, "Peace be unto you."</u>

²⁰ And when He had so said, He showed unto them His hands and His side. Then were the disciples glad when they saw the Lord.

²¹ <u>Then said Jesus to them again, "Peace be unto you. As My Father hath sent Me, even so send I you."</u>

²² <u>And when He had said this, He breathed on them and said unto them, "Receive ye the Holy Ghost.</u>

. . . .

- **THE HOLY SPIRIT IS** <u>THE SPIRIT OF JESUS</u>.
-
- **JOHN 20:19-22**
- ¹⁹ Then the same day at evening, being **the first day of the week**, when the doors were shut where the disciples were assembled for fear of the Jews, **came Jesus and stood in their midst and said unto them, "Peace be unto you."**
-
- ²⁰ And when He had so said, He showed unto them His hands and His side. Then were the disciples glad when they saw the Lord.
- ²¹ Then said Jesus to them again, "Peace be unto you. As My Father hath sent Me, even so send I you."
-
- ²² **And when He had said this,** He breathed on them and said unto them, **"Receive ye the Holy Ghost."**
-

THE HOLY SPIRIT IS <u>NOT</u> A THIRD PERSON IN HEAVEN.

Scripture:

Matthew 28:19-20 (King James Version)

¹⁹ Go ye therefore and teach all nations, <u>baptizing them in the name of the Father, and of the Son, and of the Holy Ghost,</u>

²⁰ teaching them to observe all things whatsoever <u>I</u> have commanded you. And lo, I am with you always, even unto the end of the world." Amen.

. . . .

WAS JESUS TELLING US THAT THE FATHER, THE SON, AND THE HOLY SPIRIT, ARE THREE DISTINCT PERSONS?

Answer: No!

Remember, there is <u>only one God in heaven</u>; <u>not three distinct persons in one God</u>.

THE TRUTH IS:

- JESUS IS THE ONLY GOD, YAHWEH, JEHOVAH, THE FATHER, IN HEAVEN.

- YAHWEH, JEHOVAH, THE FATHER INCARNATED INTO HUMAN FLESH AND HE BECAME THE SON OF GOD AND IS CALLED - JESUS.

- THE HOLY SPIRIT IS THE SPIRIT OF YAHWEH, THE SPIRIT OF JEHOVAH, THE SPIRIT OF GOD, THE SPIRIT OF JESUS,

THE HOLY SPIRIT IS THE SPIRIT OF GOD (JESUS), <u>NOT</u> A THIRD PERSON IN HEAVEN.

Today, JESUS is present with us in a <u>Spirit form</u> – (John 14:16). HE is <u>not</u> in person as He was while in human flesh, <u>but in Spirit</u>. We cannot see him.

THE TRUTH IS –
JESUS IS THE ONLY GOD IN HEAVEN.

1. JESUS IS THE FATHER, AND <u>HE IS ALSO</u> THE HOLY SPIRIT.

2. THE HOLY SPIRIT IS THE SPIRIT OF JESUS.

3. THE HOLY SPIRIT IS <u>**NOT**</u> A THIRD PERSON IN HEAVEN.

4. THERE IS <u>**NO SUCH THING**</u> AS THREE PERSON EXISTED IN HEAVEN.

CHAPTER 19

THERE IS ONLY ONE TRUE GOD, THE FATHER, JESUS HIMSELF – JOHN 17:1-5

John 17:1-5 (King James Version)

1. These words spake Jesus, and lifted up his eyes to heaven, and said, Father, the hour is come; glorify thy Son, that thy Son also may glorify thee:

² As thou hast given him power over all flesh, that he should give eternal life to as many as thou hast given him.

³ And this is life eternal, that they might know thee the only true God, and Jesus Christ, whom thou hast sent.

⁴ I have glorified thee on the earth: I have finished the work which thou gavest me to do.

⁵ And now, O Father, glorify thou me with thine own self with the glory which I had with thee before the world was.

. . . .

QUESTION: WHO IS THE FATHER, THE ONE TRUE GOD, THAT JESUS SPOKE OF IN JOHN 17:1-5?

Answer: JESUS.

JESUS WAS THE FATHER OF THE CHILDFREN OF ISRAEL IN THE OLD TESAMENT.

When you have a good comprehension that JESUS was the Father, the only God who spoke to the prophets in the Old Testament, you then would have no problem in understanding the words of JESUS regarding the Father in John 17:1-5.

And when you fully understand that JESUS had two natures, the human and the divine while in himself, you then can easily understand what JESUS said in John 17:1-5 in regard to the one true God, the Father.

. . . .

He that hath seen JESUS hath seen the Father. . . . JESUS is the Father.

- **John 14:6-9 (King James Version)**
- **⁶ Jesus saith unto him, I am the way, the truth, and the life: no man cometh unto the Father, but by me.**
- **⁷ If ye had known me, ye should have known my Father also: and from henceforth ye know him, and have seen him. ⁸ Philip saith unto him, Lord, show us the Father, and it sufficeth us.**

- **⁹ Jesus saith unto him, Have I been so long time with you, and yet hast thou not known me, Philip? he that hath seen me hath seen the Father, and how sayest thou then, Show us the Father?**

. . . .

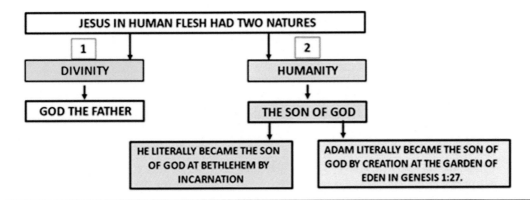

JESUS IN HUMAN FLESH HAD TWO NATURES

1 DIVINITY → GOD THE FATHER → HE LITERALLY BECAME THE SON OF GOD AT BETHLEHEM BY INCARNATION

2 HUMANITY → THE SON OF GOD → ADAM LITERALLY BECAME THE SON OF GOD BY CREATION AT THE GARDEN OF EDEN IN GENESIS 1:27.

John 17:1-5 King James Version
1. These words spake Jesus, and lifted up his eyes to heaven, and said, Father, the hour is come; glorify thy Son, that thy Son also may glorify thee:
² As thou hast given him power over all flesh, that he should give eternal life to as many as thou hast given him.
³ And this is life eternal, that they might know thee the only true God, and Jesus Christ, whom thou hast sent.
⁴ I have glorified thee on the earth: I have finished the work which thou gavest me to do.
⁵ And now, O Father, glorify thou me with thine own self with the glory which I had with thee before the world was.

NOTE: IF you had understood who JESUS was in the Old Testament, you would have no problem in understanding this statement by Him in John 17:1-5. This was the prayer of JESUS before his death. As God, he is the everlasting Father. He alone is God.

JESUS WAS THE ALMIGHTY GOD OF ABRAHAM, ISAAC, AND JACOB WHO CREATED THE HEAVEN AND THE EARTH.

GOD IS CALLED "I AM THAT I AM" IN EXODUS 3:14.

- Exodus 3:13-14 (King James Version).

THE WORDS OF MOSES TO GOD

- **13** And <u>Moses said unto God</u>, Behold, when I come unto the children of Israel, and shall say unto them, The God of your fathers hath sent me unto you; and they shall say to me, <u>What is his name? what shall I say unto them?</u>

THE WORDS OF GOD, THE I AM THAT I AM.

- **14** And <u>God said unto Moses</u>, I Am That I Am: and <u>he said</u>, Thus shalt thou say unto the children of Israel, I Am hath sent me unto you.

**JESUS SAID, "BEFORE ABRAHAM WAS, I AM"– (John 8:58).
SURELY, JESUS WAS "THE I AM THAT I AM" WHO SPOKE TO MOSES AT THE BURNING BUSH (Exodus 3:14 .**

JESUS ALONE WAS THE GOD (ELOHIM / YAHWEH / ALLAH) WHO CREATED HEAVEN AND EARTH. NO TRINITY GOD.

Genesis 1:1 – In the beginning <u>God</u> created the heaven and the earth- (KJV).

Genesis 1: 3 – <u>God</u> said, "Let there be light;" and there was light.

John 8:12 – Jesus said, "<u>I am the light</u> of the world; . . ."

John 8:58 – Jesus said, "Before Abraham was, <u>I AM</u>."

Exodus 3:13. And Moses said unto <u>God</u>, "Behold, when I come unto the children of Israel, and shall say unto them, "The God of your fathers hath sent me unto you: and they shall say unto me, What is his name? What shall I say unto them?

Exodus 3:14. And <u>God</u> said unto Moses, <u>"I AM THAT I AM:"</u> and <u>he</u> said, Thus shalt thou say unto the children of Israel, "<u>I AM</u> hath sent me unto you."

CHAPTER 20

THE MISTAKE OF MRS. WHITE AND THE PROTESTANT CHURCHES ABOUT JESUS

They did <u>not</u> know that JESUS was the everlasting Father (ELOHIM / YAHWEH / JEHOVAH) who created heaven and earth in six days. They believed that GOD the Father gave birth to a Son in heaven and called his name JESUS *before* the angels existed.

They believed in what John wrote in John 1:1 and John 3:16. Had they truly understood who JESUS was in the Book of Isaiah, who had no beginning and no end, they would not have believed in John's "<u>Two Gods Theory</u>" and "<u>the Born Twice Theory</u>" of John 3:16.

Mrs. Ellen G. White was one of the founders of the Seventh-day Adventist Church in May, 1863 A.D. She is believed to be a prophet by the Church. Her writings are believed to be the Spirit of Prophecy, as the Church interpreted from Revelation 19:10.

She wrote, …. "JESUS was the Son of God: he had been one with the Him (the Father) <u>before the angels were called into existence</u>." Patriarchs and Prophets, page 38.

Look at what she wrote about JESUS in the Book – The Story of Redemption, page 15.

- Mrs. Ellen G. White, wrote: "Angels that were <u>loyal</u> and <u>true</u> <u>sought to reconcile this mighty, rebellious angel</u> to the will of his <u>Creator</u>. They justified the act of God in conferring honor upon Christ, and with forcible reasoning <u>sought to convince Lucifer</u> that no less honor was his now than before the Father had proclaimed the honor which He had conferred upon His Son.

- <u>They (the loyal angels) clearly set forth that Christ was the Son of God, existing with Him before the angels were created</u>; and that He had ever stood at the right hand of God, and His mild, loving authority had not heretofore been questioned; and that He had given no commands but what it was joy for the heavenly host to execute." **The Story of Redemption, page 15.2.**

MRS. ELLEN G. WHITE CONTRADICTED THE SCRIPTURES.

....

STATED BELOW IS THE TRUTH ABOUT JESUS THAT MRS ELLEN G. WHITE DID <u>NOT</u> UNDERSTAND.

THE FIRST AND THE LAST. HE IS JESUS.

- Scripture:

- Isaiah 44:6 – <u>Thus saith the Lord the King of Israel</u>, and <u>his redeemer the Lord of hosts; I am the first, and I am the last;</u> and <u>beside me there is no God.</u>

- Isaiah 44:24
- [24] <u>Thus saith the LORD</u>, thy redeemer, and he that formed thee from the womb, <u>I am the LORD that maketh all things</u>; that stretcheth forth the heavens <u>alone</u>; that spreadeth abroad the earth by <u>myself</u>;
-

- Revelation 21:6-7
- [6] And he said unto me, It is done. <u>I am Alpha and Omega, the beginning and the end.</u> I will give unto him that is athirst of the fountain of the water of life freely.
- [7] He that overcometh shall inherit all things; <u>and I will be his God</u>, and he shall be my son.

....

Of course, Ellen G. White, <u>the prophet</u> of the Seventh-day Adventist Church did <u>not</u> know that the Almighty God of Abraham (Yahweh / Jehovah) who spoke to prophet Isaiah and the Old Testament prophets became human flesh at Bethlehem through Mary and is called JESUS, the Son of God.

Apparently, the Seventh-day Adventist (SDA) Church still has <u>not</u> understood it yet. And that is the reason the SDA Church continued to believe in the Trinity God which is the Triune God doctrine.

There is <u>no such thing</u> as three persons in heaven called – (1) God the Father, (2) God the Son, and (3) God the Holy Spirit.

. . . .

Dear reader, please learn of <u>THE REAL TRUTH</u> about JESUS. It's so simple. Read these charts below.

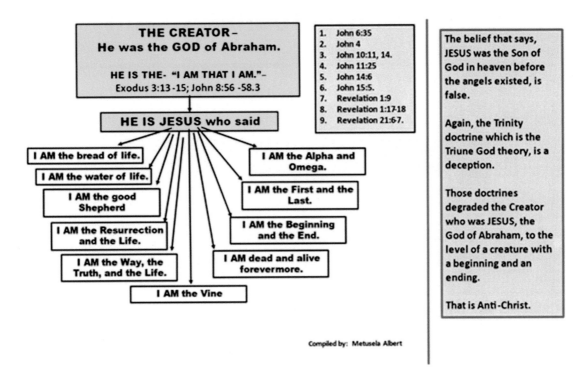

. . . .

•**THERE IS ONLY ONE GOD IN HEAVEN, AND HE IS JESUS.**

•**THERE IS NO TRINITY GOD IN HEAVEN.**

• Read Isaiah 43:10, 44:6, 24; 49:16; / Exodus 3:1314; John 8:56-58; 5:39, 46.

•**www. metuselaalbert.com**

1 **THE CREATOR – YAHWEH / JEHOVAH / ELOHIM**

2 **BECAME THE ALMIGHTY GOD OF ABRAHAM AND THE CHILDREN OF ISRAEL**

3 **HE HUMBLY INCARNATED INTO HUMAN FLESH AND IS CALLED "JESUS OF NAZARETH," THE FIRST AND THE LAST, THE KING OF THE JEWS, ALPHA AND OMEGA, THE SON OF GOD AND YET HE WAS THE ONLY EVERLASTING GOD WHO MADE HEAVEN AND EARTH.**

Read: Genesis 1:1, 3-5, 31; 2:1-3; Exodus 3:13-14; 6:1-3; Isaiah 26:4; 44:6, 24; 49:16; 9:6; 7:14; John 5:39, 46; 8:12, 56-58; Matthew 1:21-23; Luke 1:35; Revelation 1:17-18; 21:6-7.

POWERPOINT SLIDE PREPARED BY: METUSELA F. ALBERT

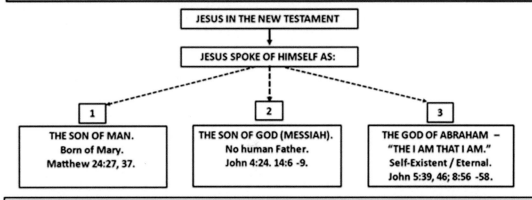

DUETERONOMY 29:29 – "The secret things belong unto the LORD our God: but those things which are revealed belong unto us and to our children for ever, that we may do all the words of this law."

JESUS IN THE NEW TESTAMENT

JESUS SPOKE OF HIMSELF AS:

1
THE SON OF MAN.
Born of Mary.
Matthew 24:27, 37.

2
THE SON OF GOD (MESSIAH).
No human Father.
John 4:24. 14:6 -9.

3
THE GOD OF ABRAHAM –
"THE I AM THAT I AM."
Self-Existent / Eternal.
John 5:39, 46; 8:56 -58.

NOTE: It is very important to understand this revelation given in the Scriptures about who JESUS was in the Old Testament; and who He is in the New Testament while in human flesh.

Prepared by: Metusela F. Albert

. . . .

Paul who wrote the Book of Acts, did <u>not</u> know that JESUS was the Almighty God of Abraham, Isaac, and Jacob in the Old Testament.

Read Acts 3:13 and understand it for yourself that Paul did <u>not</u> know who JESUS was in the Old Testament.

- Acts 3:13
- [13] <u>**The God of Abraham and of Isaac and of Jacob, the God of our fathers**</u>, hath glorified His Son Jesus, whom ye delivered up, and denied Him in the presence of Pilate when he was determined to let Him go.

This is very clear that PAUL who wrote the Book of Acts, did <u>NOT</u> know that JESUS was the Almighty God of Abraham, Isaac, and Jacob <u>BEFORE</u> his incarnation.

Unfortunately, the PROTESTANT CHURCHES of the 21 ST century A.D., still have <u>NOT</u> understood it yet.

And the <u>SDA Church</u> still has NOT understood it yet.

Unfortunately, the Protestant Churches relied on Paul's writings about who JESUS was in the Old Testament, instead of reading the Book of Isaiah. That was their mistake which made them to continue to believe that JESUS was born of God the Father in heaven. That also made them to believe in the Trinity God.

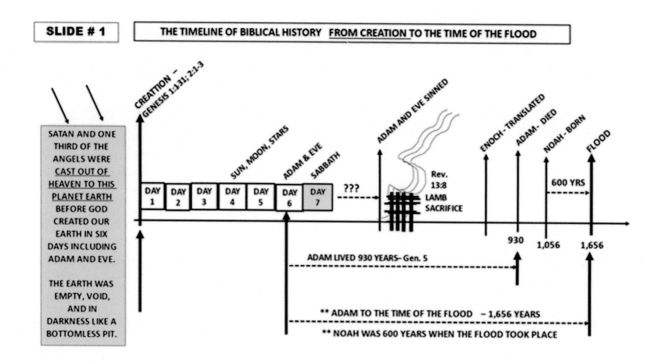

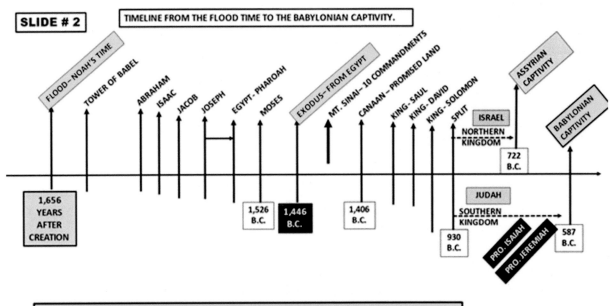

THE TEN COMMANDMETNS WERE WRITTEN BY GOD FOR ALL MANKIND   – EXODUS 20:1-17; 31:18.

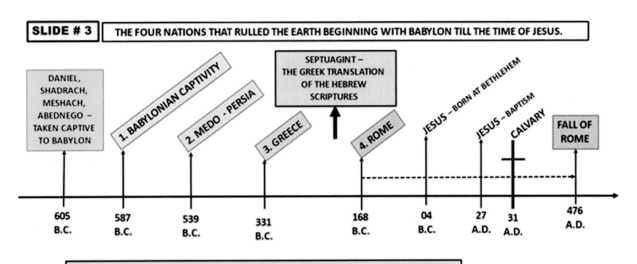

SCRIPTURE: DANIEL CHAPTER 2 – KING NEBUCHADNEZZAR'S FORGOTTEN DREAM

THE JEWISH CHURCH LEADERS INSTIGATED THE DEATH OF JESUS, AND IT WAS THE ROMAN SOLDIERS THAT KILLED JESUS ON A CROSS AT CALVARY.

NOTE: THE JEWISH PEOPLE WERE UNDER THE ROMAN GOVERNMENT AT THE TIME JESUS DIED AT CALVARY.

Conclusion

When you come to fully understand that JESUS was the <u>Elohim / Yahweh / Jehovah</u> who created heaven and earth, you then will <u>not</u> believe again in the false doctrine called – TRINITY GOD, AND TRIUNE GOD. It is that simple.

JESUS was the <u>only God</u> in heaven before the angels existed. HE created the angels. When sin took place in heaven, JESUS cast the devil and one third of the angels out of heaven to our <u>empty planet</u> earth *before* He created our earth in six days and Adam and Eve.

After Adam and Eve sinned, JESUS volunteered (as planned) to die as mankind's Sin Bearer to pay for the penalty of sin, so that none should die eternally. It was a plan He made from eternity <u>before</u> He created the angels, and our world including Adam and Eve.

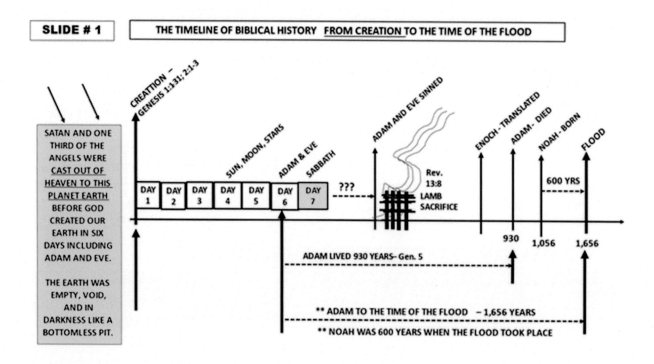

Immediately after Adam and Eve's fall, the plan of mankind's salvation was <u>implemented</u>. The Creator who was the law-giver became the Sin Bearer for Adam and Eve. No angel could become the Sin Bearer. And no baby was Adam and Eve's Sin Bearer.

JESUS who was called "I AM THAT I AM" delivered the children of Israel from slavery in Egypt. HE wrote the Ten Commandments at Mount Sinai and gave through Moses for all mankind.

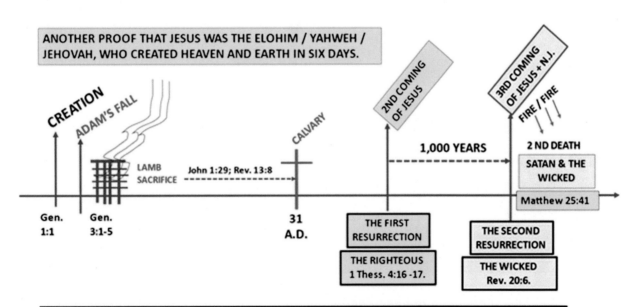

JESUS WAS **YAHWEH** WHO CREATED HEAVEN AND EARTH

YAHWEH INCARNATED INTO HUMAN FLESH AND WAS BORN AT BETHLEHEM – TWO NATURES IN HIM.

JESUS DIED

JESUS ASCENDED TO HEAVEN

ABOUT 4,000 YEARS LATER

04 B.C.

31 A.D.

31 A.D.

1. Virgin Mary gave birth to the humanity of YAHWEH which is called JESUS, the Son of God – Isaiah 7:14; 9:6; Matthew 1:21-23; Luke 1:35.

2. Mary did not give birth to YAHWEH'S divinity because God is eternal and cannot be born.

3. At Calvary, only the <u>humanity</u> of YAHWEH died. His divinity did <u>not die; for it cannot</u> die.

4. When JESUS (YAHWEH) ascended to heaven, 40 days after his resurrection, he took his humanity with him.

ANOTHER PROOF THAT JESUS WAS THE ELOHIM / YAHWEH / JEHOVAH, WHO CREATED HEAVEN AND EARTH IN SIX DAYS.

CREATION

ADAM'S FALL

2ND COMING OF JESUS

3RD COMING OF JESUS + N.J.

FIRE / FIRE

1,000 YEARS

2 ND DEATH

SATAN & THE WICKED

LAMB SACRIFICE

John 1:29; Rev. 13:8

CALVARY

Matthew 25:41

Gen. 1:1

Gen. 3:1-5

31 A.D.

THE FIRST RESURRECTION

THE RIGHTEOUS 1 Thess. 4:16-17.

THE SECOND RESURRECTION

THE WICKED Rev. 20:6.

JESUS IS "THE GOD" WHO IS COMING BACK WITH THE BREATH OF LIFE TO GIVE LIFE TO THE RIGHTEOUS DEAD TO RESURRECT IN THE FIRST RESURRECTION.

· JESUS IS THE <u>ONLY</u> GOD IN HEAVEN.

· HE IS THE <u>EVERLASTING</u> <u>FATHER</u> WHO BECAME THE SON OF GOD BY INCARNATION THROUGH MARY AT BETHLEHEM.

- Genesis 1:1-31; 2:1-3; Exodus 3:13,14; 6:1-3; Isaiah 26:4; 43:10; 44:6, 24; 49:16;
- Matthew 4:4-10; Mark 2:27-28; John 5:39, 46; 8:12; 8:58; Revelation 1:9-11; 17-18; 21:6-7.

IF YOU ARE A PASTOR,
A CHURCH LEADER, AN EVANGELIST, A BELIEVER IN JESUS AS YOUR SAVIOR,
THEN I RECOMMEND THAT YOU GET HOLD OF A COPY OF THE BOOKS,
1.   JESUS WAS THE ALMIGHTY GOD OF ABRAHAM,
2.   THE BIBLE IS NOT GOD'S WORD.

THOSE TWO BOOKS SEEN BELOW WILL ALSO HELP YOU UNDERSTAND
"JESUS IS THE ONLY GOD IN HEAVEN."

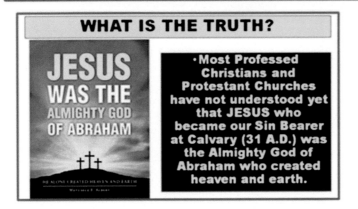

WWW.METUSELAALBERT.COM

///

Printed in the United States
by Baker & Taylor Publisher Services